ALWAYS BACK WINNERS

ALWAYS BACK WINNERS

Stewart Simpson

First published 1981
Reprinted 1994, 1995

Telephone: 01772 36720

Printed by
Cpod, Trowbridge, Wiltshire

CONTENTS

CHAPTER ONE:

How It Really Happened

The first time racing really left a mark on me was a couple of days before the 1953 Derby. I was only a lad at the time. Our scoutmaster had just put a notice up about the forthcoming camping weekend. The stupid old bugger left his hammer and half a dozen drawing pins on the bench outside the lavatory wherein I was, tightening my woggle or something. I came belting out and flopped down on the bench. The only other time I've got up so fast was when I flew out of bed on the Wednesday morning before the 1977 John Smith's Magnet Cup at York when I had just discovered in the *Sporting Life* that Ladbrokes were offering 8/1 Air Trooper.

The embarrassment after my little 'attack' will live with me for a lifetime. All the lads roaring while the scoutmaster's fat wife dabbed at my bum with surgical spirit, me jumping and starting all the while.

Naturally enough my mother went on to back Pinza in the Derby a couple of days later claiming it couldn't lose — it didn't, and everybody laughed for days at my expense. Pinza was around five or six to one and in the end I got a new school blazer out of it which must be, I suppose, some kind of rough justice.

Mentioning Air Trooper, by the way, wasn't an accident. In the compilation of material for this book I covered many horses which I have backed in recent years. As you will learn as we go on, I am not one for seeking out or raving about Derby-type horses (Pinza excepted) or classic animals at all for that matter. There are endless writings on that subject already. What I have done is to pass on a few, possibly new, ideas on racing which in my opinion offer the best possibilities for making money. I will be putting forward my case for following handicap racing — an absolute taboo among many who purport to be profit-makers at the sport.

And if, as a little tit-bit pipe-opener for you, I had to pick out an ideal horse which embodied all my ideas and requirements, then I think Air Trooper fits the bill admirably. In 1977 he won five handicaps, and in all but the first of these occasions I coined in a packet. As I will explain later, you do not need to be gambling every minute of the day to accumulate money. All you need is the right list of horses — even just a handful. The money I made from Air Trooper in 1977 would keep most folk living comfortably for a good while. Yes, just from that one horse. From the minute I saw him flying in at the finish of the Roseberry Handicap at Kempton Park that Easter I knew I was on to a good thing. Why? Because of the fashion in which Air Trooper won. There was a pack of animals all entering the last two furlongs when Air Trooper burst out and drew four lengths clear in the final furlong. What a turn of speed, and from a handicapper too. It's a sight you don't see too often, but when you do, it's time to visit the bank manager and get your cash at the ready.

On a couple of those occasions when that brilliant little horse won, hardly anyone tipped it. It makes you wonder what all the racing scribes are thinking about half the time.

It was exactly the same story when Saros, trained by Peter Walwyn and ridden by Pat Eddery, won the City and Suburban Handicap at Epsom's Spring Meeting in 1978. Nobody seemed to fancy the horse at all because of the ten stone it had to carry in the softish ground. Such a weight had never been carried to victory before in the race.

Most gamblers are so conventional you see. Very few of them try to think for themselves. They follow trends and bookies' betting manoeuvres like little sheep. If statistics or all the tipsters show that something is unlikely to happen then they convince themselves it won't. I do not believe in miracles but I *am* certainly convinced that records are there to be broken.

Although very few realised it that spring day, conditions were perfect for the four-year-old Saros to put up his record-breaking performance and I backed him with a load of cash to do just that — at the outrageous 16/1 on offer at the track. I'll tell you why.

In my book the Epsom track is a bit of a freak among racecources. It is downhill nearly all the way except for a rise just at the finish. I have found over the years that good top-weighted horses in the handicaps there have a distinct advantage over their rivals. But this was only one of the factors in Saros's favour that day. I had to call on my long memory for the others.

The first time I saw Saros was in his first ever run on a racecourse as a two-year-old. It was during the September meeting at Goodwood in 1976. I was really impressed by the way the horse sprinted away from his field in the final two furlongs to win very easily indeed. Goodwood, like Epsom, has many twists, turns, uphills and downhills. Also that day the ground was on the soft side, yielding in fact — exactly the same ground prevalent two years later when yours truly plunged in.

After Goodwood Saros went on to run a 4 length second to The Minstrel in the Dewhurst Stakes at Newmarket in October — about the most important two-year-old race in the country. Needless to say, over the coming winter Saros was looked upon as one of the class three-year-olds of 1977. The official handicappers placed him 6 lbs. (approx. 2 lengths) behind The Minstrel, the eventual Derby winner of 1977.

At three years Saros did not quite live up to the promise he had shown as a two-year-old. However, on one occasion at Newmarket, when I thought he looked a picture and ready to win, his reins broke and he finished last. He won only three minor races later that year.

Saros reappeared as a four-year-old in 1978 in the Roseberry Handicap at Kempton (one of my favourite races by the way). That day he was again a bit unlucky after a lot of barging and bumping in the straight. He finished fifth and was placed fourth after a stewards' inquiry.

Then on to Newbury a couple of weeks later. Newbury is the exact opposite of Epsom, having a long punishing straight of five furlongs or so. It wasn't just yielding that day, it was really soft, and Saros with top-weight of 9 st. 5 lbs. had little chance of winning.

These then, were all the factors leading up to the Epsom Spring Meeting of 1978. To me, a handicap man through and through, a dream come true. However, I am jumping a bit ahead of myself, and you too no doubt. Let's start at the beginning and work through the whole racing scene. By the end of the book I hope you will be on the look out for, and be able to dig out winners like Air Trooper and Saros for yourselves.

While not recommending the Pinza method for picking winners, let's get one thing straight right away — to hell with convention and other people's tips! Let's base all future plans on what we have seen with our own eyes and what we can deduce logically for ourselves.

How then does one place a bet? Unless you have been making it a point of walking around the streets of Britain with a sack over your head, you will have noticed the occasional 'Mecca', 'Ladbrokes', 'Hills', or 'Corals' in your area. These shops, in fact, stretch like a giant web over the whole nation. Indeed, they perform much the same function as the spider's web too — waiting patiently to attract then sting their victims. Unfortunately, for our operation they are, to begin with anyway, a necessary evil.

I personally find betting shops extremely depressing. They are invariably full of losers and losing, my friends, is a disease ten times more contagious than any plague the world has ever known. I spend as little time as possible in these places.

When entering a bookmaker's premises you will notice, on the wall, holders full of betting slips with carbon copies attached. On each slip you will have a place for your selection, your stake, the time of your race, and your return. Normally there will also be a small corner for the tax on your bet (a damned outrage in my opinion). The current rate of tax is 10p in every £ (or 10%). You have the alternative of paying your tax when placing your bet or waiting and having it deducted from your winnings. Obviously the goons who are regular losers seldom pay it first. I advise paying it right away because you shouldn't be expecting to lose. The little calculation below will show why:

£10 win on a 3/1 winner will cost you £10 + 90p tax = £10.90
You receive £40. Therefore profit = **£29.10**

If you wait to see if you have a return the bet will cost £10.00.
The same winner will yield £40 less 9% (£40 — £3.60)
= £36.40 — £10 stake
Therefore profit = **£26.40**

When you place your bet at the counter it will be timed, photographed, and you will receive your carbon copy as a receipt.

Some typical bets are shown below.

STAKE ● SELECTION		TIME
NIJINSKY £1 WIN		3-30 Epsom
TAX	9p	RETURN
TOTAL STAKE	£1·09	£3·00

This is a single bet (one horse only)
Nijinsky won at 2/1

Note: Betting Tax is subject to variation and in December 1981 stood at 10%.

STAKE & SELECTION		TIME
NIJINSKY RED RUM £1 DOUBLE		3.30 EPSOM 3.00 LIVERPOOL
TAX	9p	RETURN
TOTAL STAKE	£1.09	£15.00

This is a double bet (2 horses)
If one loses no return.
If two win at 2/1 and 4/1 then return is
£1 @ 2/1 = £3
£3 @ 4/1 = £15

STAKE & SELECTION		TIME
NIJINSKY RED RUM TRIGGER £1 TREBLE		3.30 3.00 4.00
TAX	9p	RETURN
TOTAL STAKE	£1.09	£52.50

This is a treble bet. All horses must win e.g. 2/1 4/1 5/2
£1 @ 2/1 = £3
£3 @ 4/1 = £15
£15 @ 5/2 = £52.50

HOW IT REALLY HAPPENED

STAKE & SELECTION		TIME
3 x £1 Doubles	NIJINSKY	3-30
	RED RUM	3-00
£1 TREBLE	TRIGGER	4-00

TAX	36	RETURN
TOTAL STAKE	£4-36	£95-50

This is known as a 'three cross'.
If any two win you have a return.

Possible Doubles
2/1 & 4/1 = £15
2/1 & 5/2 = £10.50
4/1 & 5/2 = £17.50

If all three win you have three doubles (as above) and the treble.

	£52.50
	£15.00
	£10.50
	£17.50
Total	£95.50

The following examples are 'Each Way' or 'Place' bets. With these investments you can back your selection to come first, second, third, and in some cases fourth. Bookies vary in their terms for place betting but at the moment some firms are offering as follows:

1) *Handicaps (favourite at evens — 1/1 — or odds against)*

6 or 7 runners	:	¼ win odds 1st & 2nd.
8 to 10 runners	:	⅙ win odds 1st, 2nd, 3rd.
11 to 15 runners	:	⅕ win odds 1st, 2nd, 3rd.
16 to 21 runners	:	⅕ win odds 1st, 2nd, 3rd, 4th.
22 & over runners	:	¼ win odds 1st, 2nd, 3rd, 4th.

2) *Non-Handicaps (favourite evens or odds against)*

6 or 7 runners	:	¼ win odds 1st & 2nd.
8 to 15 runners	:	⅙ win odds 1st, 2nd, 3rd.
16 & over runners	:	⅕ win odds 1st, 2nd, 3rd.

3) *All races where favourite is odds-on*

6 or 7 runners : 1/5 win odds 1st & 2nd.
8 or over runners : 1/8 win odds 1st, 2nd, 3rd.

My examples are calculated at 1/5 odds, 1st, 2nd, 3rd, for the place parts.

STAKE & SELECTION		TIME
TROY £1 E.W.		3.30 EPSOM
TAX	18	RETURN
TOTAL STAKE	£2.18	£8.00

This is an 'Each Way' bet. If your selection wins at 5/1 your return is:
£1 @ 5/1 = £6 (win part)
£1 @ evens (1/5) = £2 (place part)

Total £8

If your selection is 2nd or 3rd you receive only the place part:
£1 @ evens (1/5) = £2

STAKE & SELECTION		TIME
TROY HENBIT £1 E.W. DOUBLE		3.30 4.00
TAX	18	RETURN
TOTAL STAKE	£2.18	£72

This is an Each Way double and is calculated as above. If both selections win at 5/1 & 10/1 your return is:
£1 @ 5/1 & 10/1 = £66 (win part)
£1 @ evens (1/5) & 2/1 (1/5) = £6 (place part)

Total £72

If one selection wins and one is 2nd or 3rd your return is the place part only (as above) = £6

If the two selections are beaten but are placed (2nd or 3rd) you again receive only the place part = £6

One winner + one unplaced
NO RETURN
One placed horse only
NO RETURN

HOW IT REALLY HAPPENED

These examples I have given above are very basic indeed. Bookmaking firms offer any number of what they call multiple and speciality bets involving all sorts of selections. I must admit I don't know half of them myself and don't want to either. My recommendation for this book is stick to the first example — the single. The big firms only operate these multiple bets like the 'ITV SEVEN' and the 'BBC TRIELLA' to make a handsome profit for themselves. It is also great publicity for them when they are mentioned on TV. Take my word for it, they hate single bets and make the least profit from them. How often have you seen people cracking up with frustration over multiple bets? I must have heard the same hackneyed lines a million times — two winners out of three, three winners out of four, four out of five, and endless other twisted variations of bad luck. The one extra winner needed to make the 'big killing' always seems to let people down. You will lose hundreds of good-priced winners if you embark on the multiple bets trail. Certainly they are fabulous if they come up but like the football pools, you can spend a lifetime waiting for the big day.

Number of doubles, trebles, etc.

Number of horses	Doubles	Trebles	Accum's			
			(4)	(5)	(6)	(7)
2	1					
3	3	1				
4	6	4	1			
5	10	10	5	1		
6	15	20	15	6	1	
7	21	35	35	21	7	1

No doubt after reading this book, and in spite of my advice, some of you will use my methods and try to plunder the bookies with some of these bets. For you I have included the table above. It is an at-a-glance calculator showing the number of doubles, trebles and accumulators (i.e. foursomes, fivesomes, etc.) involved in selections ranging from 2 to 7.

> e.g. If you have 6 selections you have 15 doubles, 20 trebles, 15 foursomes, 6 fivesomes, and 1 six horse bet, giving 57 bets in all. For some unknown reason this six horse investment is commonly called a 'Heinz'.

CHAPTER TWO

Always Back Winners

In general most of the horses I back are winners. That is to say, they have won a race last time out and are in prime condition to do so again next time out. There are certain other circumstances when I back horses such as Saros (I will explain them later), but in the main the ones I go for, and which you should be looking out for, fall into this 'recent winners' category.

Many horses in training are nothing more than one-paced plodders. Of course they win races occasionally. It is obvious that if you race ten one-paced, gutless, animals against each other you will eventually get a winner. Predicting what that winner will be however, can send the shrewdest of logicians heading for the asylum.

The horses I put on my list must have two basic qualities:

(1) *The will to win* — horses are just like human beings in this respect. Some of them are half-hearted cowards that will never win a race, while others have great courage and the determination to be

winners. You must be quite ruthless in weeding the plodders out and have the guts to drop horses which show any flaws in their make-up. Some backers continue foolishly to follow bad horses because of some quirk of fate in the distant past when they nearly won a race. It's like picking the same numbers on the football pools every week. You get to the stage where you are terrified to leave a horse alone in case it happens to come in at twenty-to-one some day when you've not backed it. Believe me, these animals are better left alone. Even if they do win eventually, you can well afford to ignore them.

(2) *The power of acceleration* — again comparing horses and humans, it is the footballer or runner who can suddenly quicken and change pace who becomes the star. He soon leaves all the one-pacers behind. When a horse quickens in the last few yards to win a race you will find, given the same conditions, it can do it again. That's when the money goes down.

The Psychology of Gambling

Before getting down to the serious business of beating the bookies I think it is first essential to examine a little of what I like to call 'the psychology of gambling'. In many ways it is more important than the exercise of picking winners itself.

Anybody can pick the winners of horse races. It's happening every day from Land's End to John o' Groats. That is exactly why those bookies' shops nationwide are full all the time. I mean, you don't need a Sherlock Holmes to deduce that if people continuously backed losers then these same shops would be empty and soon out of business.

As I say, anybody can back a winner, and sooner or later a backer will hit a day when everything goes right for him and he goes home with a pocket full of cash. That's what keeps the whole show ticking over. However, if that same backer kept books of account for a year, entering all expenses for his gambling activities, even down to his daily newspaper, then it is almost certain he would be showing a loss at the end of that period. The key phrase I always use in this area is 'in the long run'. What you must always aim for is to win in the long run. Certainly you'll have disastrous afternoons. Horses are not robots and even the bravest and fastest of them can have 'off days'. In the following chapters I will set out a plan of action for you to come out on top at the end of a season and eventually take up gambling as a way of life — a very comfortable way of life. But first you must get yourself mentally prepared for the exercise. You must start believing it can be done. If you do not you will most certainly lose.

How many times during your gambling years have you been told 'you'll never beat the bookies' or 'win today, give them it all back tomorrow'? Thousands of times I'd wager. But who are these people who tell you this? I'll tell you. They are exactly like some of those horses I've just been on about — the one-paced plodders of life. They have no success, courage, or sense of adventure themselves and get their kicks by telling you how wrong you have been and how the whole world is really a massive conspiracy against the ordinary little working man. Dump these people immediately or they will drag you down into mediocrity with them. You will end up chained beside them in some moronic factory all your life while the boss is living it up at Ascot with all the champagne and birds he can handle.

If you think I'm exaggerating visit your local library and go to the biography section. Dig out books on anybody who has made a lot of cash — Onassis, Rockefeller, anybody. Adventurers and gamblers to a man.

I don't know how many times I have been travelling to and from racecourses only to hear people say 'I don't really expect to win anyway'. My opinion of these people is that they are crackers. What an attitude to adopt! Believe me they will never be winners at anything in life because they have conditioned themselves to losing.

I say honestly to you right now, that every time I put money on a racehorse, I fully expect it to win. If it does not, then there is, somewhere, a logical explanation for the defeat. I try to find it, then move on.

Believe in yourself now!

In this 'psychology' section I must also hammer another golden rule into your brain. You may find it unpleasant and maybe even unacceptable, but unless you pay heed you will never succeed in the gambling world:

NEVER MIX GAMBLING AND ALCOHOL!

I cannot stress this point too strongly. If you think I'm blowing hot air then put my theory to the test.

(1) On a Saturday afternoon when punters are falling and fumbling out of their local pub into the bookies, go along in with them and see how many people working behind the counter are drunk. You'll be lucky to find one. If a bookmaker's area manager spots any employee in a drunken state they are fired immediately. It's one of their most stringent rules.
(2) Go into any casino and see how many of the people who work there are under the influence of alcohol — nobody.
(3) If you have a decent win at your local race track, ask your bookmaker to come with you for a celebration drink between races — no chance.

All these people treat gambling as a business. It is the way they survive and feed their families. You must use similar tactics.

The Financial Side of Gambling

Let me tell you what happens when you pull off a little win in your local bookies shop. Lets pretend it's Saturday afternoon. You've had a couple of pints in the pub, browsed through the racing section of your morning paper, and come up with three horses you think have a good chance.

At about one o'clock you slip round to the bookies and lay out a quid on a three cross (three doubles and a treble). You then return to the pub or go off to watch Arsenal and forget all about your bet.

At five o'clock you are utterly astounded because the three horses have won. You have fifty quid to collect. Now your problems really begin.

(1) Your mate, who has been with you all afternoon, doesn't actually ask you for anything after you have collected your

winnings. He just looks at you with great big sad eyes. You know he is nearly skint.

"Here's a fiver mate."

"No, don't bother."

"Go on, take it."

"Are you sure?"

"Yeh, no problem."

"Okay then — em — I'll give it you back next week."

"Don't be silly — give me it when you've got it."

"I didn't really want you to . . ."

Now you've got £45

(2) Over to the 'off-licence'. Bottle of whisky and a dozen cans. Double supply of fags. Sweets and lemonade for the kids. Chocolates for the wife.

Now you've got £35

(3) "Thank goodness you had a little win today. I'll be able to get that new dress for Terry's wedding now without digging into the bank money."

Now you've got £15

(4) "Dad, I hear you had a bit of luck today. Any chance of lending me the money to get the new Wings album. I'll pay you back out of my pocket money at twenty-five pence a week."

Now you've got £10

(5) "Think I'll nick down the pub Nelly."
"May as well come with you — little celebration eh?"

Now you've got £5

(6) Monday afternoon. Last of the big spenders. Fiver treble on three favourites at Windsor.

Now you haven't even got the quid you started with!

Recognise the symptoms? I'll bet you do. It's a well worn story. But what is the alternative? I'll tell you.

KEEP YOUR BLOODY MOUTH SHUT!

Let some money accumulate. You could have broken down your £50 into £5 units and had ten single bets instead of just one, and had a real fighting chance of something mounting up. You'll never be well off shouting your mouth off about winning money. For a start, nobody except you will ever consider those winnings as anything more than 'fun-money', to be spent as soon as possible. The standard attitude is, spend it before the bookie gets it back. Nobody will even stop to consider that maybe there was just a little skill or hard work involved in picking the winners in the first place.

Take my little example above. The bookies did not get it all back. They got a fiver. You probably got about a tenner and all the other grabbing hands got the rest — £35.

If you had happened to complain on the Tuesday about being skint, the same grabbers would have informed you that gambling is a mug's game anyway.

My rule on the money side is, *keep your gambling affairs to yourself.* Nobody will have the slightest sympathy for you if you take a dive — not even your closest family. It is not malice on their part but just a lack of understanding about what beating the bookie is all about.

Many individuals find this silence extremely difficult to maintain. I mean, it's a great feeling when you beat the book in the face of all the old wive's tales and warnings you have been subjected to throughout the years. It's good to let your friends know what a fox you are. It's even better to throw money around and show off. Everybody enthusiastically goes along with the circus — until the money runs out that is. It is then you find out what a lonely business gambling can be. Try borrowing money from a friend or relative to continue your betting and see how far you get.

Be very discreet about your racing activities.

Tools of the Trade

As with any other business you will have to lay out some cash before you can swing into action. I have laid out some basic requirements below. Do not be put-off by this initial investment. You are embarking on a new career. Organisation and readiness are essential for future success.

(1) *Sporting Life* (daily racing paper) or *Sporting Chronicle* (daily racing paper). Find a place at home to store them for reference purposes.

(2) *Sporting Chronicle Handicap Book* (weekly — 40p). Retain the pull-out sections giving previous weeks' results. Make a folder for them out of a cardboard box.
(3) (optional) *Raceform Up-To-Date Form Book* (a record of all previous year's results. 1979 Flat edition £7).
(4) Give up a night at the pub and rent a video recorder (optional of course) Great for recording races until you can afford to give up work (approx. £3 per week).
(5) A Bank (absolutely essential). This relates to the previous paragraphs on money. The amount available for your bank must, of course, depend on what you can afford. The rule to use right across the board, however, is only to bet one twentieth of your total bank at any one time. You can start with as much or as little as you like. For example:

£20	= 20 bets @ £1	single bets only
£40	= 20 bets @ £2	
£400	= 20 bets @ £20	

(tax not included in this example)

When your bank doubles then double the stake. That is, when your £40 becomes £80, raise your bets to £4.

If you hit a bad run and your £40 becomes £20, then half your bets to £1 and so on.

It takes a long time to get cleaned out using this method and it ensures a cushion for a bad spell. I would add, however, that if after reading this book you actually bet twenty or so losers in a row, I think you should seriously consider taking up gardening or running a boy scout troop.

You will be pleasantly surprised how your bank will grow, and, as I have previously advised, you should treat your money like a business investment. Do not be down-hearted about not winning too much at the one go. If, for example, you bet £2 on a 2/1 winner you will receive (before tax) £6. This may not appear to be very much, but lets look at exactly what has happened. You have laid out £2 and received twice that amount in winnings which is a 200% return on your investment. There would be something close to the great Yukon Gold Rush if terms like that were offered on the

London Stock Exchange for a two minute investment. I suggest you lay out your bank like this:

Stake	*Return*	*Actual Winnings*	*£40 Bank (£2 bet)*
£2.09 (tax paid)	£6 (2/1)	£3.91	£43.91
£2.09 (tax paid)	loser	none	£41.82
£2.09 (tax paid)	£10 (4/1)	£7.91	£49.73
£2.09 (tax paid)	loser	none	£47.64

N.B. When you are starting out your operation pay the tax on bets before you put them on (currently 9p in the £). When you actually go racing you cannot do this. Bookmakers at the track automatically deduct 4p in the £).

If you cannot afford a bank to start with then save one up at two or three pounds a week. It is essential not to be betting on an all or nothing basis. Winning at horse racing requires a great degree of patience and saving for a few weeks will do you no harm. During this time you can be thinking over some of the recommendations I am putting forward and preparing a new list of horses to watch out for. Just tuck away the money you would usually be losing each week until you have £40 or £50.

CHAPTER THREE

Where To Begin

Now down to some nitty-gritty. What type of racing should we concern ourselves with? It is most certainly impossible to cover it all. If you think you can effectively take in all the information from every distance of race at every meeting summer and winter, forget it. It has been my experience, both with my own efforts and in observation of others, that this cannot be done. There are just too many facts and figures to absorb and a body can end up departing completely from reality in a mass of statistics and useless activity. It is a good idea not to have too wide a field to cover. To sit back occasionally, relax, and reflect on what's going on is of great importance. If you are active in every race, every day, you will end up broke no matter what kind of run of success you may hit. Eventually you will slip up, maybe just through tiredness, the point being, where gambling is concerned, you get no second chances.

Two businessmen friends of mine illustrate this point well. They both gamble in hundreds of pounds, sometimes thousands. They are at it every single day trying to cover the whole spectrum of horses, dogs, casinos, and private card games. Yes, they win thousands from time to time, but regularly I meet them and they are absolutely skint. I actually had to lend one of them money for his train fare back to London from Sandown Park one day. Yet some of the winners that chap digs out are brilliant — he most certainly has talent. But at no time whatsoever does he have a long term plan for his gambling operation. With him it literally comes into one hand and goes flying out the other. He regularly acts the big shot at the track after a big win. The bookies encourage him — what a great guy he is. Can you blame them? He keeps them all in a grand life style with cash which, at the end of the day, comes from his business.

So where do we draw the line for our field of operations. Let us consider all the horse racing throughout the year.

National Hunt Racing

I always give the same answer to anyone who asks me why I never get seriously involved in this department of racing. I tell them to go some day to a 'jump' meeting and wander right down the course to one of the fences while racing is in progress. Along come the horses and over they go — twigs, branches, leaves, mud, horses and jockeys flying around everywhere. To me it is a frightening sight. You don't really notice these things when you are sitting comfortably by your telly in mid-winter. Even in the racecourse stands viewing is somewhat limited. Get up close to it and you will soon change your mind about putting your hard-earned cash down on the outcome of such a precarious business. And something else. I cannot think of a more soul-destroying or negative pursuit than spending a whole evening studying form, going racing the next day a substantial distance from home, only to see your selection hitting the deck after only a couple of fences.

Take the average jump jockey. In the course of his racing life he will break nearly every bone in his body. He will be eternally stuck in hospitals for weeks recovering from this and that. How much can we possibly depend on this nonsense?

Sorry! National Hunt is out for this project.

Flat Racing
(Two-year-olds)

Anyone connected with trying to evaluate the form of two-year-olds will tell you that it is one of the most difficult areas in racing in which to achieve accuracy.

Basically these two-year-olds are the babies of racing. Many of them do not really realise what is required of them until their third or fourth years, after they mature considerably. A great number of races for these animals are for newcomers that have never raced before. Maybe a stable will have an idea that a two-year-old will win first time out. After all, they can be galloped against older horses in a yard to find an approximation of their ability. Even then there are many gambles on such horses that fail miserably. You in your local bookie's shop have no idea what has gone on behind the scenes at stables. Neither have you a clue what shape these young horses are in as they walk round the paddock at the track. Many people use the betting market to gauge the chances of two-year-olds but I can assure you, following the betting market blindly is suicidal. A backer can fall into many traps by doing this. If making a profit was simply a case of following betting manoeuvres there would not be a bookie left in business. Think about it.

Two-year-olds are horses all developing and maturing at different rates. Trying to follow form with such animals will have you tearing your hair out in no time.

Two-year-olds out!

(Three-year-olds)

Much of what I have said already about two-year-olds applies to three-year-olds in the early part of a season. Often even horses that have shown ability at two years do not develop (train on) over the winter and retain that form the next year. Remember Tromos in 1979? Winter ante-post favourite for the Two Thousand Guineas and reckoned by one and all to be in the Mill Reef and Brigadier Gerard class, the horse was soundly trounced in a three runner race at Newmarket in his first outing as a three-year-old. He never raced again and was a bitter disappointment to everyone concerned —

especially many professional backers who had plunged heavily on him.

My rule for three-year-olds is to only back them after they have run and won at that age. Naturally, of course, they will also have to have shown the attributes which I require before I back any horse.

It is a good idea to let the three-year-old form settle down for a couple of months, until about June. This is not a stringent rule however. Occasionally early on in April or May you may spot a horse which has the qualities we are looking for.

(Older Horses — Four-year-olds and upwards)

This, in my experience, is where the money lies. At the beginning of the season this is where all your efforts should be concentrated. Why? Because with four-year-olds we have animals which have been, in most cases, racing for two seasons. We have plenty of information about them. We know the distances they prefer, the ground conditions, and sometimes the tracks suitable for them. It does not require a genius to see what kind of advantage you have following these horses as opposed to two-year-olds. There is just no comparison. Winning at gambling is about having the information available on which to base our investments. Why base them on unsubstantiated guesswork? Isn't it far better to have a sound backing for our conclusions in the form of past records and reports and what we have seen with our own eyes? Of course it is.

Distances

What distance of races should we then go for? Again we have a tremendous amount of information to take in if we are going to cover every distance available from 5 furlongs to 2 miles plus. Is one distance better than another? I believe so. My rule is, limit operations between 7 furlongs and 1½ miles, the ideal distance being 10 furlongs (1¼ miles). Why?

Let us take an average 5 furlong race at Kempton Park which has a separate straight course for sprints of this kind. The standard time for this distance is 59 seconds. Let us break that down a bit:

5 furs. = 59 secs.
1100 yards = 59 secs.
18.64 yards = 1 sec.
55.92 feet = 1 sec.

Amazing isn't it? Yes, these animals cover approximately 56 feet in a second. The shorter the race the more hectic it becomes. At 5 furlongs the horses go flat out from start to finish and it is easy to understand that if a horse stumbles, misses the nod coming out of the stalls, or gets bumped somewhere along the way, then it has a hell of a job ahead trying to get into a challenging position never mind actually winning the race. Add this to a bad draw at the stalls and you are really in trouble.

Never back in 5 or 6 furlong races!

Once you reach the 7 furlong and mile area you have a situation where that break out of the stalls is not just as vital and in my opinion the skilled jockey has more time to manoeuvre and actually use his talent. Many people use time calculations for 5 and 6 furlong races and there is a certain amount of logic in it, but the whole operation depends on clear trouble-free runs. Many times in horse racing you do not get that important prerequisite.

Even 7 furlong and mile races can become a bit of a dash when they are run on straight courses such as Newmarket or Doncaster. (I will go into this difference in racecourse structure later).

How about the longer races?

My most important requirement in a horse is that it wins its race by producing acceleration in the final couple of furlongs. I believe that, in general, longer distance races do not throw up enough winners with this vital turn of foot. Certainly there are a few, especially in the real big money top class events such as the Ascot Gold Cup run over 2½ miles. You will find often though that you cannot get a decent price for these animals because there are so few around.

Many times these long races are competed for by one-paced plodders that have basically failed at all other distances. We must limit our operation somewhere and I think it is wise to stick at around 1½ miles as our longest distance.

Class

What class of racing should we aim at? To answer this question I must first explain how horses are rated in this country.

The official handicappers rate all horses here on a scale of 0-100. Each horse is allocated a rating in pounds relating to its performance on the racecourse. For example, Troy, last year's Derby winner, was rated 96 — the best horse in the British Isles. That is an exceptional rating and few horses ever reach this level on the official scale. Troy had to win both the English and Irish Derby's, the King George VI and Queen Elizabeth Stakes at Ascot, and the Benson and Hedges Gold Cup at York to achieve this rating and quite frankly horses of such a calibre appear only rarely. Another problem as far as our scheme is concerned is that as soon as a horse like Troy establishes his true merit, it is very difficult to get any sort of reasonable price about him for future events. Where on the scale do we seek our winners then?

A rough estimation of the handicap scale is something like this:

Rating			
80-100	Horses in this bracket are the highest class animals and will be competing for the 'Group' races. That is —		
	Group 1	Derby	Classics
		1000 Guineas	Classics
		2000 Guineas	Classics
		St Leger	Classics
		Oaks	Classics
		Benson & Hedges	
		King George	
		Arc de Triumph	
	Group 2	e.g. Big Ascot & Goodwood races	
	Group 3	e.g. Classic trials at Sandown, Chester, Epsom etc.	
70-80	Some Group 3 races and top handicaps e.g. Royal Hunt Cup at Ascot, John Smith's Magnet Cup, York. Newbury Spring Cup. The Lincoln, Doncaster.		

60-70	Top and everyday handicaps at the better meetings.
40-60	'Bread and butter' handicaps at all tracks throughout the country.
0-40	Lower class handicaps and Selling races throughout the country.

The plan of action I am recommending is to make our field of operations in the 50-75 bracket — the good handicappers, always, of course, with a weather eye open for something suddenly improving from the 45 region.

Why not the highest class animals?

As I mentioned with Troy, once really top class horses show their greatness no decent price can be got for them. Also, and especially nowadays, these huge prizes are competed for by horses from Ireland and France. It is very difficult indeed to draw conclusions from this unrelated form until the horses have actually raced against one another. Do not be taken in by all the ballyhoo that precedes big races like the Derby and the Guineas. Much of this euphoria on the part of the press, TV, owners, and trainers, is due to the great stud values at stake when winning these great races. If an owner's horse wins a classic at 4/6 he receives a giant prize and a guaranteed couple of million from the Americans for the animal to go to stud there. Great of course for the owner — for us, a bad investment, taking into consideration the risks involved beforehand with all that attempted pulling together of form from three different countries.

At the bottom end of the handicap scale things are even more bleak. The selling races for instance, where the winner is put up for sale after the race, attract the very poorest and slowest of animals. Trying to find winners among this lot will most certainly find you broke at the end of the season — long before that in fact. As with the two-year-olds, a stable will occasionally have a good thing lined up for a seller. However, the chances of you and I knowing about it are very slight.

No sellers please!

Maiden races, for horses that have never won, are much the same.

Trying to dig out winners is extremely hazardous when you are faced with a field where the horses *have* actually run two or three times before and still failed to win a race. I am always very wary of backing horses that have not proven they can win.

You have probably read or heard "smart-alecs" saying 'never bet in handicaps'. This is the biggest fallacy in racing and I'm sure a story put round in the first place by bookies. Nearly all the money I have won personally has come from handicap racing and the goons you hear knocking it haven't a clue what they are talking about.

What exactly is a handicap then?

It is an exercise whereby the official handicappers try to give all the horses in a race a chance of winning by allocating them greater or lesser weights according to their ability. The theoretical aim is for all the horses in a handicap to finish at the winning post exactly in line: That never happens of course, but often we have photo-finishes throwing up some really close things. There are rarely any more than two or three horses involved though.

The general opinion most people adopt is that after the handicapper has done his work the chances of finding winners become very small. I take exactly the opposite view. I use the conditions of these handicaps for my own ends.

When you think about it in depth you soon realise that in a handicap all the horses are chained into a kind of theoretical compartment which, most of the time, is difficult to break out of. Once an animal proves that it *can* break out of this strait-jacket by producing a good burst of speed, then I take note of it immediately with a view to a future bet. Remember, there should be no hurry to throw your money around. Just wait patiently for the right horses to come along and back them again when the time is right. Your bank will start creeping up steadily and healthily.

In these races which I am recommending, the handicapper is actually stopping the biggest majority of the horses for you, especially the one-pacers that cannot accelerate at all. Once these animals are properly rated (and at four years the chances are that they will be) it is extremely difficult for them to win again. You will often notice them running up continual seconds and thirds but never actually breaking out of that 'strait-jacket' and getting their noses in front. Sometimes they are actually backed favourite on the strength of these placings — all great stuff for us.

The horses with a 'turn of foot', as it is called in racing parlance, are not around every day, but what an advantage they have. To my mind this is one of the very few flaws in the British handicap system that can, if used properly, give the backer a substantial edge over the odds. If, for example, a bunch of horses all enter the final furlong together and one suddenly accelerates and wins by a length then he will be handicapped for his next race on that one length victory. However, the trained eye in the stands, as you will become, will have noticed that the horse had a ton in hand at the end of the race and that the animal will more than likely be under-handicapped for some future event — that's when the cash goes down, sometimes at ridiculously high prices.

I must throw in a couple of warnings at this point before I go on. Finding your small list of good acceleration horses is not all that must be done to ensure success. You must wait until conditions are right for them to use their speed to the best advantage. For instance, a horse that has shown his speed qualities over 10 furlongs may just find 12 a little too much for him. He has no strength left with which to accelerate in the last yards of the longer race. Always aim to back a horse to do something it has done before.

Another problem concerning a horse's ability to quicken is the overall pace which a race is run at. There is in racing a group of horses in the 70-80 calibre which I like to refer to as 'high class plodders'. These animals are frequently placed in top races — maybe even sixth in the Derby or fourth in the Guineas. They are quite genuine but have no quickening powers. One thing they can do however, is run a race in a fast overall time, maintaining the same gallop throughout. Sometimes these gallopers can knock the guts out of our good accelerating handicappers, especially on straight courses. I never back these horses to do this but it is always necessary to be wary of them. We must try to make sure that our selections are not outclassed and given too much to do.

CHAPTER 4

The Structure of Handicaps

Now let us have a look at how handicaps are constructed and arrived at in the daily racing papers. It is very important to read the small print at the head of each race. In this preamble the conditions of the race are set out. In our handicaps, beside the title of the race, the prize money, and the entry fees etc., you will notice a few words and figures indicating the standard of the horses allowed to take part. It will read something like this:

'for four-year-olds and upwards — rated 0-60'

or

'for three-year-olds only — rated 45 plus'

Remember the official handicap scale I mentioned earlier? Applying this to the above examples is self-explanatory. In the first case only horses up to a rating of 60 can enter for the race and in the second, only horses rated over 45 can compete.

Why is there a need to segregate horses like this? Well, it is simply to cater for a wide range of animals giving them, at some time or another, a chance of winning. Obviously if all the handicaps were open-ended, then some horses and owners would never win anything. After all, there are far more moderate animals in training than there are champions, and if the sport is to survive, even as entertainment in some cases, we need them all. The system of handicapping gives all types of horses a chance of picking up a prize.

Before I go on let me set down what I believe is the most important fact in handicap racing. It relates to horses being allocated different weights.

Weight can slow horses down but it can never make them run any faster than their own ability allows.

Never forget that!

I will explain further. Let us suppose we have a horse (rated 70) one day winning a mile handicap race at Ascot carrying 9 stone, and in doing so, breaking the course record.

The second horse (rated 70) was beaten 4 lengths. It also carried 9 stone.

Obviously, before the race, the handicappers were of the opinion that both of these horses were of the same ability (rated 70). Hence the same weight. However, after the Ascot event a new assessment would have to be made, especially in view of the fast time, or in racing jargon, a 'truly run race'. Over a mile the official opinion is that 3 lbs. in weight equals one length in distance. Theoretically, our winner has improved to the tune of being 12lbs. better than the horse it beat into second place. This is not uncommon by the way. Horses can improve as much as that, sometimes quite unexpectedly.

Two months later the same two horses meet again at York. Our winner is now rated 82 and carries 9 st. 12 lbs. The Ascot second is still rated 70 and again carries 9 st.

What will the outcome be assuming they fill the first and second places again?

Again theoretically, they should finish in a dead-heat. But as often as not (given the same ground, which would have been on the firm side) the record-breaking animal will win again. Why? Because giving the second the extra weight allowance will not make him run any faster. He could run every week for years and still not equal the other horse's Ascot time.

The outcome of my little example would depend on whether the fastest horse could be slowed down or not.

If you imprint this into your brain you will go a long way to understanding handicapping.

If our Ascot winner had won producing a good burst of speed then a page of my notebook would have been devoted to him. We would really have been on to something there. My example, of course, is purely imaginary. Ascot course records are not broken too often, especially by handicappers. But try and remember that little rule always:

Weight can slow horses down but it can never make them run any faster than their own ability allows.

Earlier I suggested operating among the horses rated 50-75, that we keep our eyes open for horses in this bracket winning their handicaps by accelerating in the final furlongs. Once we have spotted a horse though, when is the ideal time for it to win again? Obviously we want the same distance as when it impressed us. We want the same ground if possible. If our animal shines on firm ground, then we have to be very careful if it encounters soft when unproven on this ground. But leaving these well-defined needs aside, where and when should we make our move in relation to how the horse is handicapped? Personally, I prefer to wait until the horse is among the top-weights in a future handicap. Then it will be encountering rivals of lesser ability, many of them having no quickening powers at all. We must always beware of those 'high class plodders' making the overall gallop too severe.

Being a top-weight is not a must however, and there are certain circumstances that occur when it is beneficial to back horses in the bottom half of the handicap. This is usually when a horse wins a good class handicap convincingly and is out again within a short time. If a horse wins a handicap, say, this Saturday, and is out again next Saturday, then it will carry what is known as a penalty. In the sporting press it is usually shown after the horse's name as (3 lb ex) or (5 lb ex). This penalty is incurred because the handicappers have not had time to re-assess the horse. The entries for next Saturday's race have been made some time ago. The penalty is added to the horse's weight in lieu of a new rating. Quite often this extra weight is not enough to stop the horse winning again.

I am not suggesting for a minute that you blindly back all animals carrying penalties, but if you find one of your short-listed flyers with good quickening powers falling into this category, then it is something else again with which to back up your own findings.

If you think you have spotted a good 'un from a lowly handicap, be careful not to ask it to do too much next time. Jumping from a Folkstone 0-60 to an Ascot 50 + is just asking for trouble. Your horse may well be a future top-notcher but try and confine your bets to like races or, at the most, the next grade up.

Chart 1 *Flat Racecourse Groupings*

Group 1	*Group 2*
Ascot	Brighton
Ayr	Chester
Doncaster	Lingfield
Epsom	Redcar
Goodwood	Ripon
Haydock	Salisbury
Kempton	Thirsk
Newbury	
Newcastle	
Newmarket	
Sandown	
York	

Group 3	*Group 4*
Bath	Catterick
Beverley	Carlisle
Chepstow	Edinburgh
Hamilton	Folkestone
Leicester	Warwick
Nottingham	Wolverhampton
Pontefract	
Windsor	
Yarmouth	

Chart 2 *Rising Grades of Races* (a purely personal chart)

0-40
0-50
0-60
30-60
0-65
30-65
35-65
0-70
30-70
35-70
30-75
35-75
35+
40-70
40-75
45-75
40+
45+
50-75
50+

Above are two important charts. The first is the official grouping of British racecourses. The second is my own personal table showing the different grades of races. These charts will give you a good indication of what your horses have to do as they move up and down the various tracks and handicaps. Remember, as well as taking into account the difference between, say, a 0-60 handicap and a 50+ handicap, you must also consider the different standards of racecourse. For instance, there can be a vast difference between 0-55 at Newmarket and a 0-55 at Carlisle, if only by the nature of prestige at both courses. I am in no way maligning the Carlisle Racecourse, but I think when you are considering investing your hard-earned cash on racehorses, all factors must be recognised and taken account of.

Many people get thoroughly confused when glancing through handicaps in their daily paper. They fail to understand why one day a horse will have top weight and another day, bottom weight. It is not really so difficult to work out once you know what's going on. Let us again create an imaginary horse. We shall call it Wee Sammy. It is rated 50 on the official scale.

Now if this animal is entered in a 0-50 handicap it will be allotted top weight. Its rivals' ratings will probably vary between 30 and 50 and they will be weighted accordingly. Below is an example:

THE SIMPSON HANDICAP, one mile, two furlongs;
£2,000; for four-year-olds and upwards — rated 0-50

(Rated)		Age	Weight
50	Wee Sammy	4	10 0
43	Big Jenny	5	9 7
40	Tiny Willie	6	9 4
36	Uncle Fred	4	9 0
33	Auntie Jessie	4	8 11

(5 runners)

As you can see Wee Sammy is the top-weighted horse because he is top-rated at 50 by the official handicappers. To give his rivals an equal chance, they have all been weighted below in conjunction with their official rating.

Now let us assume that Wee Sammy is entered for a better class handicap worth £7,000. He could then find himself at the bottom of the handicap thus:

THE STEWART HANDICAP, one mile, two furlongs;
£7,000; for four-year-olds and upwards — rated 50 plus

(Rated)		Age	Weight
71	Lovely Leslie	4	10 0
65	Nosey Jimmy	5	9 8
60	Silly Billy	4	9 3
55	Big Fanny	5	8 12
50	Wee Sammy	4	8 7

(5 runners)

As I mentioned earlier, given both opportunities, I would, providing he was on my list and I got around 3/1, back Wee Sammy on the first occasion. He has lesser horses to beat there whereas on bottom weight, as well as being able to accelerate, he would have to be able to out-gallop his superior rivals. Lovely Leslie and Nosey Jimmy, for example, are reckoned to be 21 lbs. and 15 lbs. better (7 lengths and 5 lengths at level weights) and once you reach the 70's territory, you are in the region of very decent horses. You must always consider the class of each race and make sure your selection has a fighting chance.

I will show you how to pull all these suggestions and ideas together when I cover my 'typical season' in the Appendix. But first the racecourses. Most racing publications have a bit about this shoved into the last couple of pages. I cannot allow this because racecourse structure is vital to our operation. Wee Sammy's case in the more valuable race mentioned above may not be all that hopeless if you take into account the track the race was to be run on. If, for instance, it was to be run over the Newmarket Rowley Mile Course where there is a straight 10 furlongs, then Wee Sammy's low weight could well be an advantage. Lovely Leslie's ten stone might just floor him. Maybe the four with heavier weights cannot accelerate. All these things have to be reckoned with before the money goes down.

With all this in mind then, let's consider the racecourses.

CHAPTER 5

The Racecourses

You may remember that in Chapter Two, I mentioned other circumstances when I backed horses. Well, this is in direct relation to certain racecourses which, I believe, offer a substantial advantage to the horses placed with most weight at the top of handicaps. These are what I call the turning tracks. My belief is an elementary one. If horses run on a straight course, it is an entirely different kettle of fish to racing over one with bends in it. To take extreme examples let us consider the straight 10 furlong course at Newmarket against the 10 furlong course at Chester — the smallest course in Britain.

At Newmarket the horses are faced with a great wide, windy, expanse of land around them. They tend to set up a severe gallop throughout and many animals have the guts knocked out of them long before the finish. Some horses are particularly suited to this type of race — especially the big powerful plodders. Sometimes these animals defeat their rivals by sheer elemental brute force. There is no acceleration involved at all and every pound of weight really counts. In these conditions good horses can be slowed down by allocating them big weights. Their powers of quickening can be cancelled out.

The Chester course, on the other hand, is round and only just over a mile in circumference. In the 10 furlong course (actually 10 furlongs 24 yards) the horses have to negotiate no less than four bends. In fact, apart from the short 2 furlong straight, they are more or less turning all the time. Few horses can ever go flat out on this compact little course and in my opinion the top-weighted good class animals have a distinct advantage. They can canter along until the last couple of furlongs then deliver their challenge. The weight they have been carrying has been no burden at all. Don't let us forget why they have top weight in the first place. It is because, on known form, they are the fastest horses.

How can we use this knowledge then? I myself always consider these top-weights very seriously, especially when a leading jockey is booked for them. Naturally I still require a horse with guts and determination but I am prepared, on certain occasions, to forego a little finishing speed.

With this in mind then I will go over the racecourses of Britain. On some courses certain numbers at the starting stalls have an advantage. These positions are drawn for the day before racing. In large fields this obviously becomes more important. I have included this information for you.

Ascot: Group One: Right-Handed

I go to nearly every Ascot meeting. The standard of racing is excellent. Because owners and trainers go overboard to have winners there, especially during the Royal meeting in June, you are guaranteed first class competition from the best horses.

I normally go by car but there is an excellent train service from London's Waterloo Station. Be careful though, it is quite a little hike from the station up to the main road. If you want a taxi you have to get out of your train like greased lightning. Some of those big fat bookies have the scene all sussed out. They know exactly where on the train to sit so they can get off to a flyer for the taxis at Ascot Station. I remember one day getting into a bit of a wrastling match over a taxi with, among others, Clement Freud the MP. After a lot of grunts and wriggles seven of us ended inside one taxi. I was lucky enough to be knocked down into a seat. Clement got one too. Many F's and C's later three of the gorilla's had to bow out and we finally got going. We could have walked to the course in the time it took to sort out the passenger list.

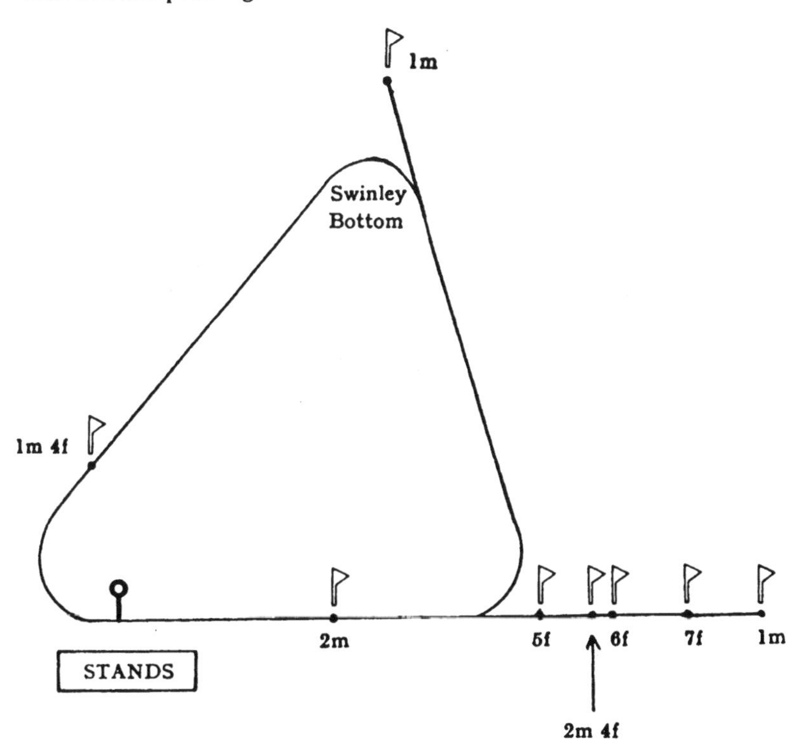

Although Ascot has quite tight bends on the round course, I do not believe any horse has a weight advantage there. From around Swinley Bottom the course is rising all the time until about a furlong from home. I can never make up my mind about this round course. I really think it depends on the tactics used in each race. For instance, sometimes the mile course (old mile) looks rather easy, especially when a field dawdles from Swinley Bottom to the bend into the straight. Then we are left with no more than a three furlong dash to the line and the acceleration horses appear to have a big advantage. On the other hand, even with the bend, the horses sometimes set up a tremendous gallop, many of them finishing absolutely exhausted. I think you have to try and work out beforehand how each race is going to turn out before plunging in with the cash. If the ground is heavy I advise you to keep your money firmly in your pocket and wait for another day. In heavy conditions it is quite a gallop altogether.

The straight mile is a much stiffer course even although there is a slight descent at the start. From the five furlong pole it is uphill nearly all the way.

While there are many key races at Ascot over a season, one in particular is vital to our operation. It is the Royal Hunt Cup, run on the Wednesday of the Royal meeting in June. This race is one of the most important handicaps in the whole racing calendar. It is run over the straight mile and is usually contested for by all the top class handicappers specialising in that distance. Normally every horse is tuned up to do its best and although we may not even back anything in the race, much important information can be gleaned from it. Some of the horses in the first half dozen may be ready shortly afterwards to win easier and less competitive events on turning tracks. If it is at all possible, I recommend a visit to the track for this race if only to make paddock observations. (I will cover this topic later).

If there is any edge at all here it is with Lester Piggott's mounts. He is the undisputed master at Ascot having recorded nearly twice as many winners as his nearest rival Willie Carson. Lester knows every blade of grass on this course and if he is engaged for any of my short-listed horses, I get the cash down without any hesitation.

All the stands at Ascot offer excellent viewing and it is a very comfortable track in general. Something you cannot fail to notice, however, are the many little doors and balconies you are not allowed into. These are watched over passionately by doddering elderly officials who look as they are guarding, with their lives, the last bastions of the British Empire.

Draw Over the years I have come to believe that the draw is of little importance at Ascot.

The BBC coverage of Ascot is excellent and the big Royal Meeting is an ideal event for the video.

Ayr: Group One: Left-Handed

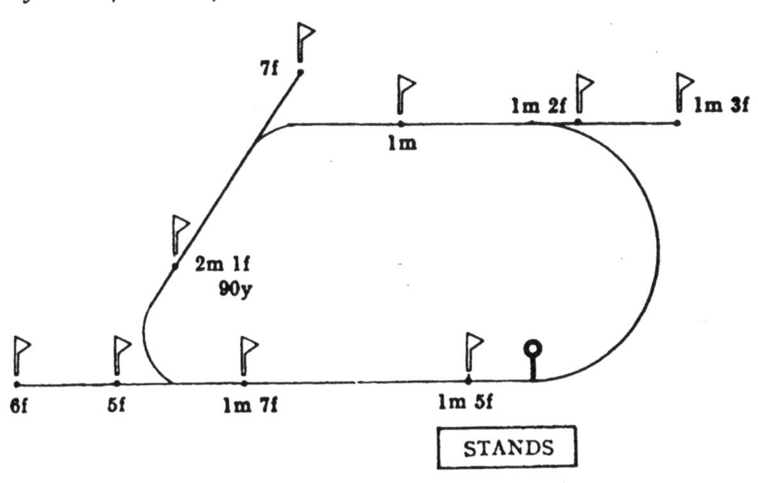

When I lived in Glasgow I naturally used to visit Ayr often. Nowadays, though, it invariably clashes with one of the big Southern meetings and my only trips up there are usually planned to coincide with visits to my relatives. I like the town of Ayr itself. Being a holiday resort, you have all the pleasures of the town at your disposal after racing — and many a 'braw bricht moonlicht nicht' I've had there too. A great place for drinking and dancing. I must admit that my stringent rules about alcohol finish as soon as racing is over. The last time I visited Ayr I had to be, shall we say, assisted to my hotel room by the local constabulary. And damned understanding they were about it too, considering I had no trousers on at the time. It was all because of that fast bitch I got tangled with; I had an idea she was too smart by far from the minute I set eyes on her in the Members' bar after the last race.

But that day, quite unexpectedly, I spotted a little horse that was to bear plenty of fruit in the future — Tesoro Mio. I'll tell you about him later.

Ayr is the only Grade One course in Scotland. In fact, over the flat, there are only two others in Edinburgh and Hamilton. Lanark closed a couple of years ago, which I think was a great pity considering the shortage of tracks up there. When you think of the glut of racecourses we have here in the South, it's a bit of a liberty. I mean, as far as I can see, people in Scotland are just as keen on their racing as their southern counterparts. With North Sea Oil and all making the North East of Scotland a bit of a boom area, a racecourse around Aberdeen would not go amiss. Possibly a conversion of the National Hunt course at Perth could be the answer. I can tell you, there's some load of gambling goes on up in the Aberdeen area. I'm convinced there is a fortune waiting there for some enterprising smarty.

Ayr is a big wide track suitable for any kind of horse. The four furlong galloping straight and easy bends rule it out for any advantage to the top weights. For any of our quickening animals though there is ample room for a late burst.

The view from the stands is excellent and it is quite a refreshing change to hear the Scots accent throughout the place. Often some of the imposters in the South get on my bloody nerves.

Draw In races of 7 and 8 furlongs the low numbers may have a slight advantage although a high one wouldn't stop me backing a fancied runner.

Bath: Group Three: Left-Handed

Setting out to Bath from London is quite an undertaking. I think for a day's racing the car is definitely out. British Railways' express trains to the West Country get you down to Bath Spa in about one and three quarter hours. You then have to take the local bus through Bath and up to the racecourse, situated high above the town some eight hundred feet or so above sea level. The exercise, as well as being tiresome, is costly.

The course itself is just in excess of one and a half miles and rather severe, rising steadily and bending all the time during the last four furlongs. With Group Three racing and its lower class of handicap, there is no guarantee whatsoever of leaving the course in pocket unless you actually fancy something. The course is within reasonable reach of the Lambourn training territory and top trainers from that area such as Peter Walwyn, Barry Hills, and Dick Hern, run many of their lower class newcomers there. Racing for newcomers does not concern me and I rarely go to Bath. Obviously, if you live near the course, then it is well worth a visit. Bath is a lovely place and the course is rather quaint.

On my most recent trip there I missed the last train home. I had been drinking in the early part of the evening and found the town a bit dull. However after missing my train, resigning myself to it, and seeking out some further entertainment for the night, I found the place quite lively later on. I got home three days later.

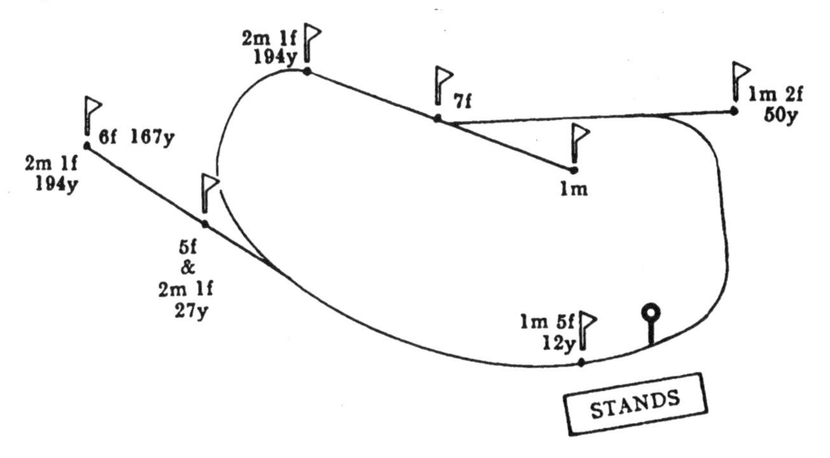

The stiff nature of the straight nullifies any weight advantage for us there. Do not make the mistake of comparing Bath with Chester. Although they are both turning tracks they differ considerably.

Draw With the course continually on the turn, low numbers have an advantage in races up to one mile.

Beverley: Group Three: Right-Handed

Beverley town is altogether too religious looking for me. Bloody great church buildings everywhere. It's a busy enough little haunt though — a market town full of hustle and bustle. I was last up there in 1976 and in the morning before racing I visited one of the historical holy places and said a few prayers just in case. It certainly did no harm. The horse I had taken a fancy to, and travelled there to back, won at 13/8. I got 2/1 myself. Lord Helpus was its name. Ironic wasn't it.

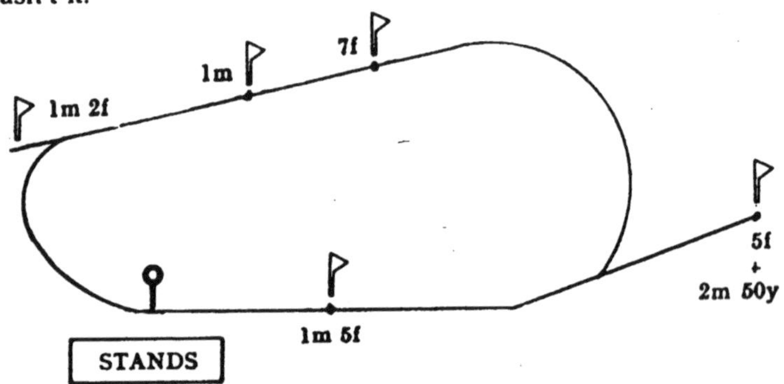

The course is just over one mile three furlongs in extent and is quite a test of stamina — especially in the soft. The straight is partly uphill and has a bit of a bend in it about two and a half furlongs from home.

Draw High numbers are best here.

Brighton: Group Two: Left-Handed

I have always regarded Brighton as London by the seaside. It is so busy and easily accessible from the Capital that many people actually commute between London and Brighton daily. The train service from Victoria is excellent and there is a good bus service from the station to the course. For goodness sake don't walk it. I did once and my shins were aching for days. The course is on top of a steep hill by the way.

I occasionally go down to the Brighton races. Now that the nudist beach is in full 'swing' I will make it a point of going down more often. I mean, the racegoer is in an ideal position in this respect. A brisk walk along the promenade with Sporting Life tucked under the arm and the Brighton Members' badge tied to a lapel. Who's going to think the binoculars as anything else but normal?

I'm not really surprised that Brighton should lead the field in nudist pursuits. Time and time again at parties down there I've found people more than willing to take their clothes off. There is plenty of night life in Brighton and loads of pouting continentals.

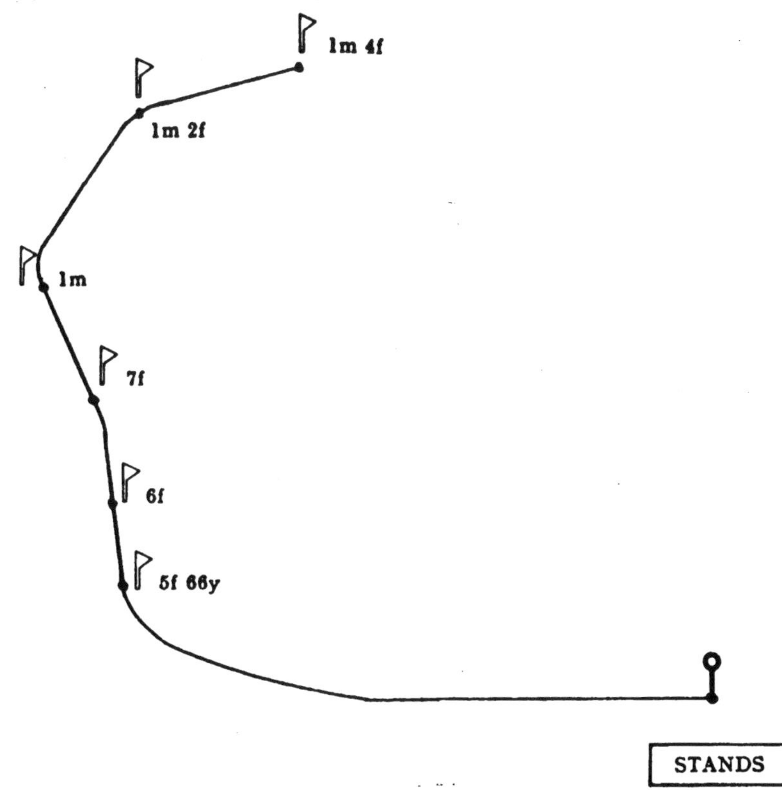

STANDS

The racecourse, though, is a lovely little place and perfect for a day out if you get fed up goggling at all those tits and bums. There is one thing at Brighton however, that can ruin a day's sport — the sea mist. On two occasions I've been there the mist has come swirling in and blanketed out the whole of 'Race Hill' where the track is situated. One day I left a sun-drenched cloudless London and made my way to the coast only to find the dreaded mist swirling around the track in Mount Everest fashion. The pantomime that followed was hilarious. After the 'off' of each race everyone just stood and chatted until the horses burst out of the gloom about a furlong from home. Nothing else at all was visible. The commentator's 'I can't quite pick them out at the moment' had everyone, including myself, in stitches.

On another occasion Bert Lynch and the whole of the 'Z cars' team arrived to film one of their TV episodes. There was good fun that day too.

Some really nice pubs in Brighton and if you are an antiques person, then, as well as racing, you can spend endless hours browsing around all the junk shops.

The racecourse is one and half miles long and extremely tricky. I believe however, it is a good course for exploiting the top-weight theory. The track sweeps downhill for a long stretch and weight is not difficult to carry there. You often find that horses that win at Brighton become course specialists there. A couple that spring to mind immediately are Perucio (five races there in 1976) and Hang on Elvis (five races in 1978). In many ways the Brighton track resembles Epsom. There is a rise to the winning post from about two furlongs out.

The stands at Brighton are very steep and a good view can be had by one and all. Always take some eye protection with you there — either sunglasses or a brimmed hat. On good days the glare from the sun and the sea is quite overwhelming.

Draw Because of the sharp turns in the track, low numbers drawn on the inside rail have a bit of an advantage.

Carlisle: Group Four: Right Handed

Any time I've visited Carlisle I've always felt a bit guilty. The place is full of dirty great walls built specifically to keep wild northerners like me out. 'Strengthened against Scots' was a term I saw somewhere in the city. A bloke in a bar there told me that long ago they used to have a curfew after which no Scotsman was allowed to roam around the place — a damned outrage don't you think? And bad luck on the publicans.

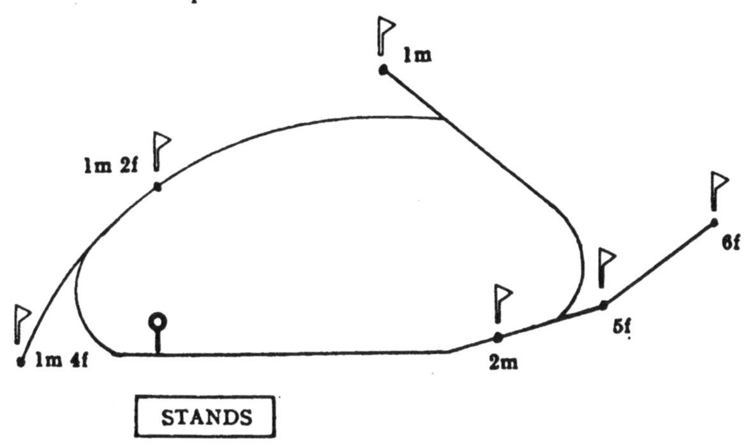

The course is over a mile outside town and, being at the very northern tip of the Lake District, is extremely picturesque. It is quite a stiff track, about one and a half miles round with slight undulations and a substantial stretch of the straight uphill. There is a separate sprint course for the five and six furlong races which bends into the straight.

There is no benefit for weight-carriers here and it is essential that any horse you back has no stamina problems, especially in softish ground.

Draw The high numbers are best at Carlisle, more so in the sprint races.

Catterick: Group Four: Left-Handed

Catterick is a small sharp course just over a mile in circumference. It has many undulations and a horse must be quite agile to negotiate the track. Top weights, in theory, should do well there but very often success depends on individual horses and jockeys rather than any track advantage. There is a nearly-straight five furlong course.

As with any other Group Four course, it is far better to go there to back a horse which has taken your fancy rather than trying to dig one out when you get there.

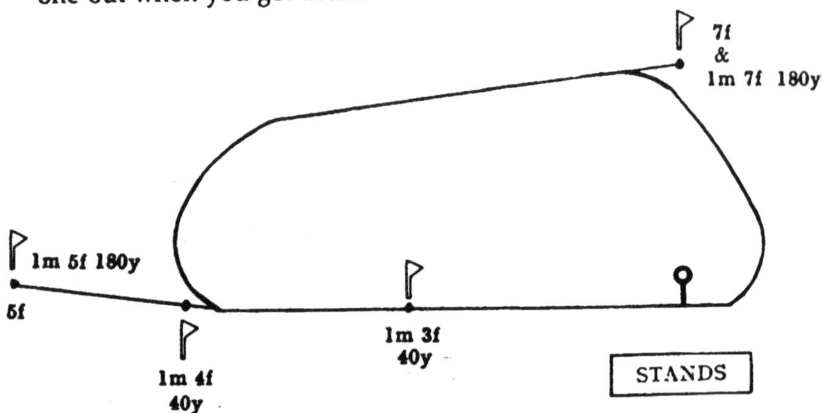

Catterick is very popular with Northern racegoers and big crowds are regular. Personally I will never forget the place. Once when I was there a group of soldiers standing beside me at the paddock asked if I thought one of the horses walking round had a chance. I was all dressed up that day and they must have thought I was in the 'know'. The race was a 'seller' and some of the horses would have had difficulty pulling a milk cart. The soldiers' particular fancy had run ten times the previous year, failing to make any impression whatsoever on the form book. I laughed and forwarded my theory about the horse seeking employment with the local dairy. The brute quite naturally won at 25/1 and I spent most of the meeting locked in the toilet while the troops scoured the course for me. I didn't stay long in the town that night either if I can remember right.

Draw The low numbers are favoured slightly on the five furlong course but have a definite advantage on the round track.

Chepstow: Group Three: Left-Handed

Chepstow is the only Welsh flat racecourse and it is just inside Wales and no more. It is about a mile from the Severn Bridge. The course is very picturesque and extremely hilly. If it weren't for the severe undulations it would probably be deemed a galloping track being two miles in length with a five furlong straight. I don't quite know what to make of Chepstow. Probably the nippy agile horses are at home there although the long run-in could be against them too. Maybe its better to assume that all horses have an equal chance there. Our top-weights certainly don't have anything in their favour.

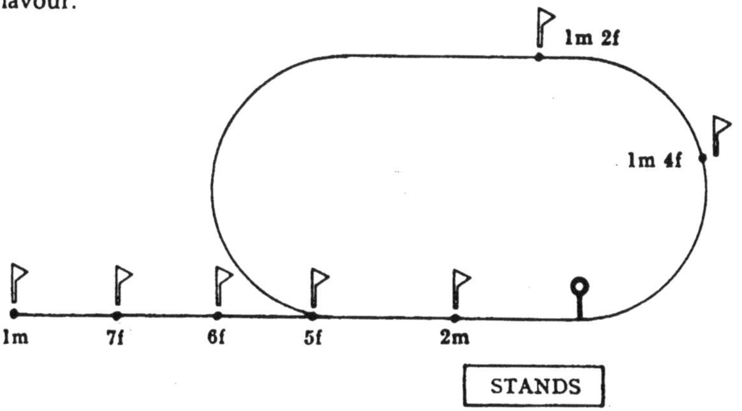

1m 2f
1m 4f
1m 7f 6f 5f 2m
STANDS

I always feel that Chepstow is a far better jumping venue (Group Two status) than a flat racing one. Sometimes though, the Lambourn trainers send decent horses to the track.

Whenever I meet up with Welsh people I always seem to have a great time. On my last visit to Chepstow I ended up sleeping in a van just outside Monmouth with a rock group. Great entertainers the Welsh — especially those all-female outfits.

Chester: Group Two: Left-Handed

Although most of my activities are confined to the South nowadays, I always plan to take in the Chester Spring Meeting. It is a must for the keen racegoer. The course has only Group Two status but this May fixture is as near Group One racing as you'll ever get.

As I explained before the Roodee, as Chester is called, is the smallest circuit in Britain. It is just over one mile long. The top-weight theory is very relevant to this track. Although extremely sharp, the course is perfectly flat and a good experienced animal should not really be inconvenienced. It's a good idea to follow the top jockeys there. Regularly they dominate the big May meeting.

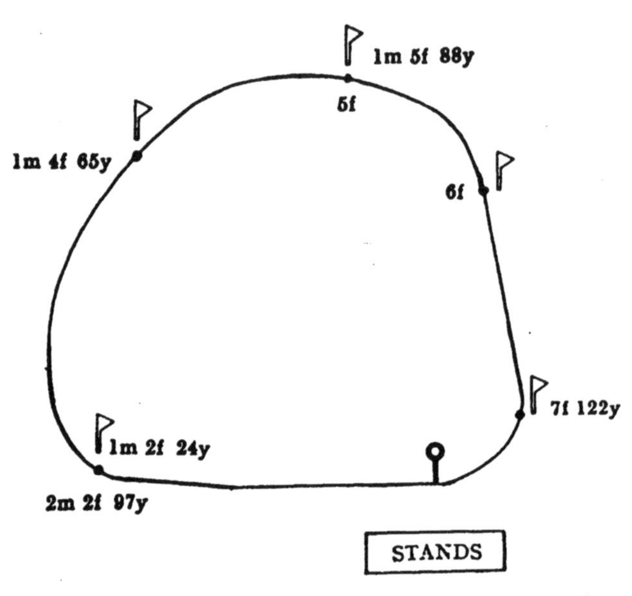

After racing you could not find yourself in a cosier wee place than Chester. The inner town, surrounded by the City Wall, is quite enchanting with its old wooden-beamed period houses. The Cheshire people are very friendly — a fact which lured me into a rather bizarre situation one night.

Down in a pub on the banks of the lovely River Dee I started chatting to a bloke and his wife who were seated beside me at the bar. He had noticed my sporting paper and the conversation that followed centred around Sea Pigeon, the Chester Cup winner of that day. At closing time the bloke asked me if I would like to go to a little party with them to meet a few friends whom, he said, were dead keen on the Turf. Terrific says I.

The little party, in an old musty house not far from the centre of town, turned out to be some sort of séance. I found myself, just after midnight, holding hands with everyone in a stupid circle in the centre of the living room. I don't really know that much about the procedure in séances but when they all started chanting for the Devil to appear, I got off my mark sharpish. You never know, there may have been some kind of sacrifice on the menu. I was the only stranger. To hell with that!

The memory of them all howling after me that night as I made a bee-line for the door, still crops up in nightmare form now and again — after a heavy night on the curry usually. But the next day I was back to my old self and I backed a nice top-weighted winner at 7/1 — Casino Boy, trained by Ryan Price and ridden by Brian Taylor.

Apart from the occasional Satanist here and there, Chester is a great place for winning money.

The BBC's coverage of the May meeting is excellent.

Draw Naturally with the track being so tight the draw is important at Chester, particularly in the shorter races. Low numbers are best. However, nothing is sacred in racing; Casino Boy, mentioned above, was drawn ninth of twelve.

Doncaster: Group One: Left-Handed

The St. Leger, run at Doncaster, is even older than the Epsom Derby. However, nowadays, the course is nothing like it used to be years ago. Escalating stairs, lifts, indoor betting facilities, and excellent viewing, are all laid on for a day's racing. The track is nearly two miles round and a galloping one, being flat with long sweeping bends. Doncaster suits any kind of horse and the four and a half furlong run-in is quite punishing for weight carriers. There is a straight mile where the horses usually set up a strong gallop. The 'Lincoln' at the beginning of the season, and the first big handicap of the year, is run on this straight course and with the large field it usually attracts, the draw becomes vital. Time after time high numbers fill the placings in the Lincoln while numbers 1-10 rarely get a look in. This draw factor makes the winter ante-post betting for the race a complete farce. Don't be drawn into it no matter how keen you are for the season to get under way.

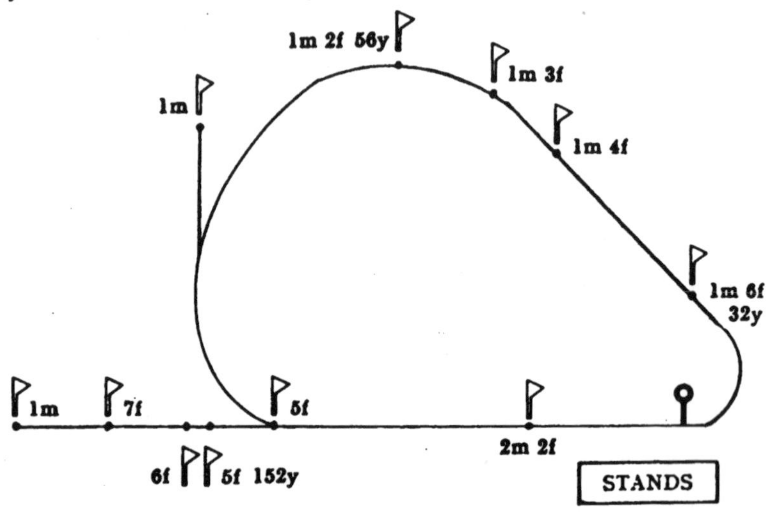

I usually only go up there for the Lincoln or St. Leger meetings. Other Doncaster fixtures always clash with important Southern meetings. The town is very busy indeed and one of Britain's commercial centres. There are numerous coal mines in the surrounding area and many mining lads make the race meetings important dates on the social calendar. The St. Leger meeting is usually packed out and it's a good idea to book a hotel room in advance. One year I just went there on spec and ended up living with a bloke who worked in a sweet factory that specialised in butterscotch. The stuff was all over the house and I remember I returned to London badly in need of dental treatment.

Draw Very important on the straight mile — especially in big fields — high is best. On the round course there is little to be gained in the draw.

Edinburgh: Group Four: Right-Handed

Edinburgh racecourse, like Folkestone, is not actually in Edinburgh at all. The course is situated about five miles outside town at Musselburgh. You can get a bus out from the centre of the City.

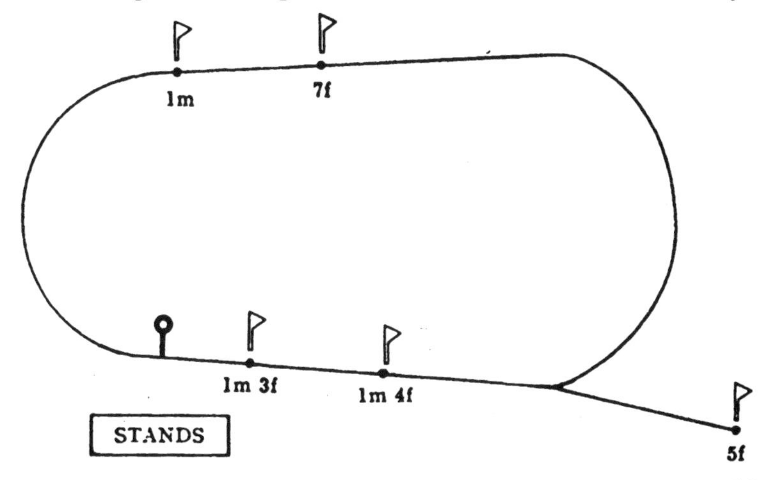

The track is just short of one mile two furlongs and, as you would expect, rather sharp. There are minor undulations. Top weights have a definite advantage here although with Group Four racing you must be certain before you back a horse that it has proven ability. In many lower class handicaps throughout the country you regularly see the same horses competing against each other. Time and time again a different winner emerges from the same bunch of horses. This is the surest sign of mediocrity. As I say; to venture into Group Four racing you must have a horse that has either been dropped in class and has proven ability, or has impressed you previously because of its quickening powers and is a cut above the others.

Edinburgh is one of my favourite hunting grounds in Britain. The castle, high on a rock above the city, gives the place an air of great strength and purpose. I always eat and drink twice as much as usual when I go there.

I particularly enjoy the area around the 'Royal Mile' which leads up to the Castle Esplanade. During the Edinburgh Festival period in late summer the pubs up there are full of interesting and sometimes extraordinary people. I was going to mention the group of Turkish belly-dancers I got in tow with one night, but for the sake of decency, I don't think I'll bother.

Draw In races of seven furlongs and a mile high numbers are best. On the five furlong sprint course high again have the advantage.

Epsom: Group One: Left-Handed

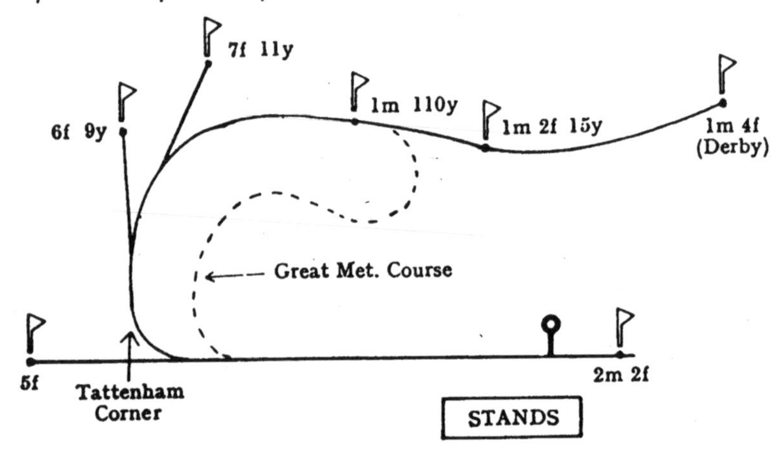

Because it is very near my home in London, I go to all the fixtures at Epsom. There are only three meetings a year taking in nine days racing in all:

April Spring Meeting	(3 days; Tues. Wed. Thurs.)
June Derby Meeting	(4 days; Wed. Thurs. Fri. Sat.)
August Bank Holiday Meeting	(2 days; Mon. Tues.)

Needless to say, the Derby Meeting is the most popular, but I myself prefer the Spring Meeting. It is one of my first major dates of the year and an ideal event to get the winter blues shaken off. As often as not I have a gamble in one of the handicaps, like my effort with Saros in the ten furlong City and Suburban Handicap. Even as I am finishing off these chapters I have pulled off another little coup with Sea Chimes. Like Saros, he also humped 10 stone to victory in the race.

You must always consider very carefully the top-weighted horses at Epsom. They have a distinct advantage there because, as I have already explained, the course is downhill for a long stretch. The course can be a bit tricky though and doesn't suit all horses. As well as being uphill and down dale longitudinally, the course also, in the straight, slopes down from the stands rails to the other side of the track. Often you will see horses hanging in towards the far rails as they try to negotiate this slope. Stewards' inquiries to sort out the bumping and boring are not uncommon.

Epsom Downs is a huge expanse of public land and there is nothing to stop you going for a wander round the course in the morning before racing. I have done this often. One time I actually ran part of the course myself from the high seven furlong start down to Tattenham Corner. I must say it is quite a gradient and it was difficult enough for me to stay balanced never mind a great galloping racehorse. Obviously the animals that win there have to be very nimble and able to handle the undulations.

I often wonder what the horses actually make of Epsom on Derby day. After their peaceful training quarters it must be an incredible experience for them, galloping up the straight with tens of thousands of loonies bawling their heads off on either side. Bravery, it seems to me, is another vital prerequisite for Epsom during the big meetings.

If you fancy a trip to the Derby I strongly advise you to get there early. Last year, the year of Troy's Derby, the traffic on the roads heading South from London was the worst I've ever known. I eventually ditched the car a few stations before Epsom and got the train the rest of the way. It was really unbelievable. The traffic was crawling at five miles an hour a long way before Epsom causing many cars to overheat, clap out, and make the situation even more desperate. You know those open-decked buses you see all along the side of the track at Epsom? Well, I saw one of them arriving from London at three forty five that afternoon. The revellers in the top deck looked really sick and a bit foolish too. Their well-planned office day out had ended up in total disaster. The first three races, including the Derby, were over by the time they got there.

I don't think I will ever attempt to go to Epsom by car on Derby day again. The train is by far the best method. There are three stations all within easy reach of the course:

Epsom Town	(bus to the course)
Epsom Downs	(walk over the Downs)
Tattenham Corner	(Walk along the side of the course)

During Derby week there is, as well as racing, a full-scale fair adjacent to the track. It is one of the year's major venues for Britain's gypsies and they gather on the Downs in their hundreds, all trying to sell their wares and make a fast buck. Some of the side-shows and stalls are hilarious but you must always be on the alert for pickpockets and con-men. I am not throwing suspicion on the gypsies in particular here. As with all huge gatherings of people, including cup finals and rock concerts, you always have to look after number one and be particularly protective towards your wallet.

The ITV do an excellent job in covering the Epsom races.

Draw As you would imagine, the draw is significant at Epsom. In races up to about a mile, low numbers are best.

You will notice on the plan of the Epsom track the 'Metropolitan Course'. This is used to facilitate only one race a year — The Great Metropolitan Handicap, run over two and a quarter miles during the Spring Meeting. The horses actually run down the track away from the stands for the first part of the race. They then head across the open Downs, which is temporarily cleared, and join the course proper up on the far side.

Folkestone: Group Four: Right-Handed

Folkestone is the kind of place that is absolutely delightful on a good day and very exposed on a bad one. The course is not actually in Folkestone at all but at a little spot, Westenhanger, six miles inland from the port. On race days the main line trains from London's Charing Cross (approx. 1½ hrs.) stop there and the racecourse is only a couple of minutes walk from the station. There is a camping site beside the track, and on certain days campers can see the racing free. Many continentals make use of the place in transit to France.

I go down there occasionally if there is a good top-weight running in one of the handicaps on the round course. Again, because of the turns and the short run-in of two and a half furlongs, the top-weight theory can be put to good use there. The straight six furlong course is very undulating indeed.

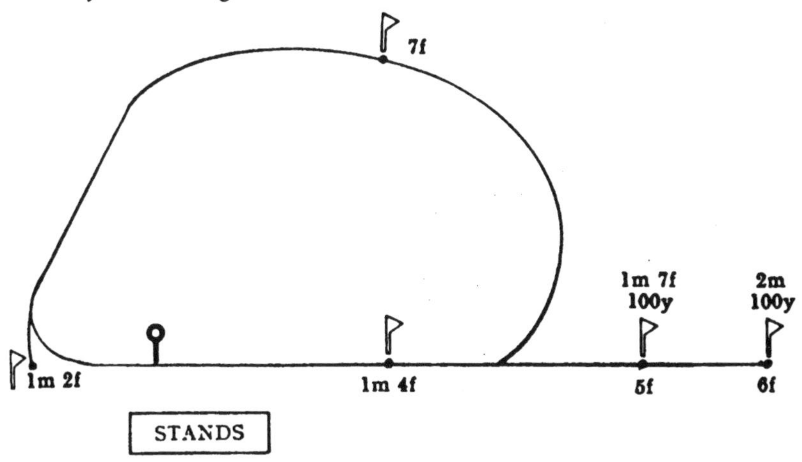

As I say, it can get very stormy down at Folkestone. I remember one day in particular I got a right old soaking. The dark grey clouds came sweeping in from the coast and the place was practically washed out. A brand new pair of suede moccasins I had bought were completely ruined. However, most of the time during the summer months, the course is bathed in brilliant sunshine. There is nothing I enjoy more than a successful day at Folkestone, a fast train back to Charing Cross, and a T-bone steak and bottle of wine in town to round things off.

Draw I don't think there is much in it at Folkestone.

Goodwood: Group One: Right & Left-Handed

If you want your racing to include brilliant scenery then Goodwood is the place to go. The countryside surrounding the course is unequalled in beauty and during the breathtaking short journey from Chichester railway station, there are times when you wonder if the local bus will actually make it up the tree-lined road to the stands. If nothing else the Goodwood country air will do you a power of good, and many people from the surrounding towns make Goodwood a picnic day out.

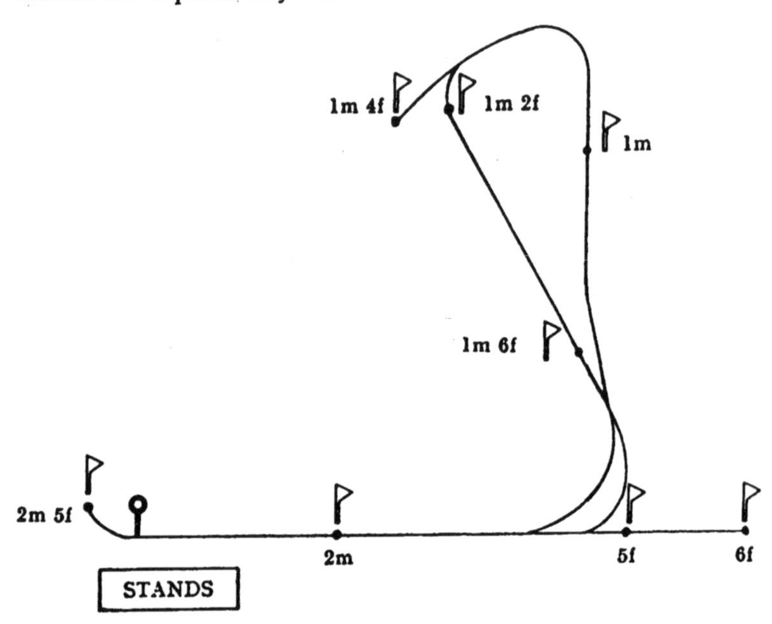

Like Epsom, Goodwood has many twists and turns and in the long distance races the horses gallop away from the stands down the course to the loop and then come back up the straight at the finish.

As far as we are concerned, we must again consider the top-weighted animals. The horses rarely go flat out until they turn into the straight and often we are left with a sprint over the last four furlongs.

Sometimes I feel that the trainers who train on downland turf, such as those at Sussex and Lambourn, may have a slight edge at Goodwood.

I go down there often although it can be a very tiring experience travelling to and fro each day during the big July five day meeting. I usually book a hotel down in Chichester for the week.

Chichester is a busy town during the day but rather quiet at night. During the July week though there are many private functions arranged by racing people for their friends. I've been to many a boozing session down that way although one night I got a bit too tight and was the subject of an attempted mugging on the way back to the hotel. July 1975 it was, in the early hours of the Sunday morning after the last day's racing. It must have been the binoculars that attracted them to me. Two black-leathered jackals from motor bikes leapt on me and knocked me to the ground. One of them reached inside my jacket to my inside pocket. There was plenty in there too. A couple of good top-weights had gone in that day. Anyway, from nowhere a big brute of an alsation appeared barking its head off and the two barbarians got off their mark, roaring away down the dark lonely streets on their bikes. Damned if I know who that dog belonged to. It just licked my hand and slinked off. Something I'll never forget was the lovely studded leather collar it had round its neck. There was a bright red jewel of some kind sewn into it. The other thing which came in handy that night was the zip I had across my inside pocket. You can't be too careful when carrying readies.

The BBC always covers the big July meeting.

Draw For us there is no significance. However, some five and six furlong backers tell me that high numbers are best on the sprint course when there are big fields.

Hamilton: Group Three: Right & Left-Handed

The layout of Hamilton is not unlike Salisbury except that at Hamilton there is a loop at each end of the track. The course is hilly and just after the dip into the straight, about three and a half furlongs out, there is a steep climb to the winning post. In spite of the twists and turns the course does not offer any advantage to our top-weighted handicappers. The stiff long straight takes a bit of getting, especially in soft ground. The six furlong course is straight throughout.

Hamilton was raised from Group Four to Group Three status a short time ago and the standard of racing has naturally risen.

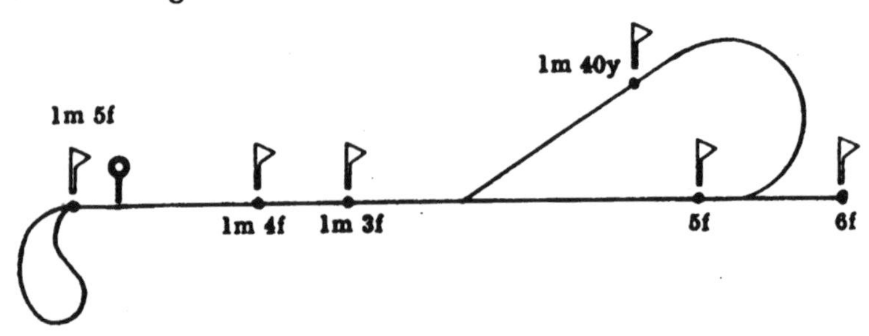

The course is only ten miles from Glasgow and the 'blue train' gets you there in no time. As with Ayr, I combine trips to Hamilton with visits to my relatives.

Because of re-development the centre of Glasgow has changed dramatically in recent years and many new interesting pubs have cropped up in the city. Being my home town, I know the place backwards. A visit to a Rangers or Celtic football match is always good for a laugh if you are in town. But beware of the derby matches between the two. Either wear blue and join the Rangers crowd or green and join the Celtic men. If you wear neutral colours like purple with yellow spots, you'll be written off as a traitor no matter what side you end up with.

The Glaswegians are extremely generous though and a body can spend endless nights in good down-to-earth boozing company. I always have a great time in Glasgow.

Draw I don't think there is much in the draw at Hamilton although high numbers are deemed best in the straight sprint races.

Haydock: Group One: Left-Handed

Haydock is one of the most important venues in the North, and many excellent meetings take place there. With the closure of Manchester racecourse in 1963 and only a few race days at nearby Chester, Haydock has become the main racing attraction for the vast populations of Liverpool and Manchester. The track is half way between these two great cities, only yards from the M6 motorway. Big crowds regularly turn up at Haydock particularly for the Saturday meetings.

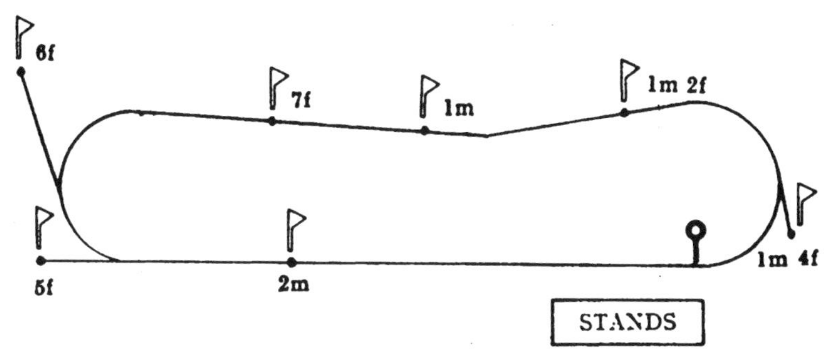

The track is about one mile five furlongs round and has a long punishing, slightly rising, straight. As you would expect, the top-weights there really have to be able to carry their lead.

Any time I am up that way I either go into Manchester or Liverpool for the evening. And great centres of entertainment they are too. Obviously an evening football match in that part of the country is a must.

Draw On the six furlong course, which starts on a shoot off from the round course, low numbers are said to be best. However, in the other races the draw would not put me off backing a fancied runner. There is plenty of room in the long straight for the horses to get into good challenging positions.

Kempton: Group One: Right-Handed

Kempton Park is one of my favourite courses. Like Epsom and Sandown, it is not far from my home. The main thing that attracts me to Kempton are the middle distance races for the older horses. Year after year at the Easter meeting I spot animals there which bear fruit later on in the season. You must always try to make it to the first Kempton meeting even if you just take notes. I go to various meetings there when I don't gamble at all. It is something you will have to consider too. In race-reading much more logic can be exercised if you have no financial involvement. The minute even fifty pence is laid down you become biased and more likely to ignore facts. This of course is where the video comes in handy. Once the passion of a race has died you can look at it again more coldly and clinically.

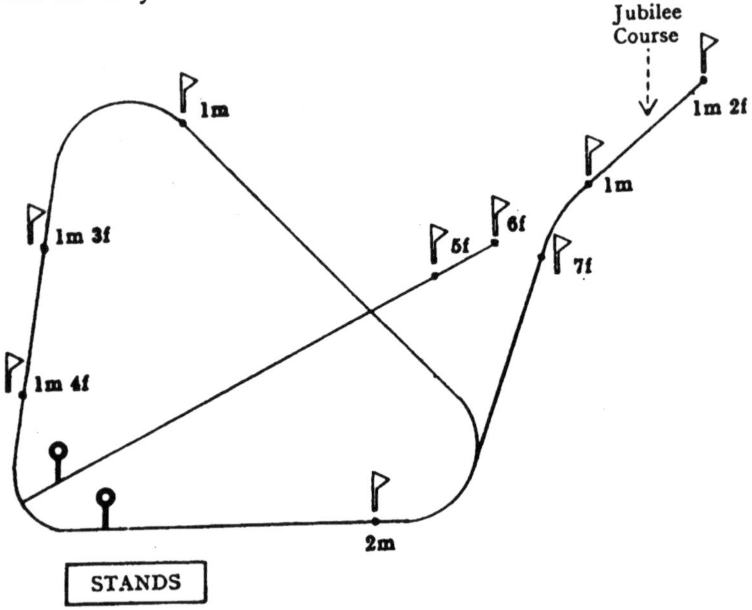

For the middle distance races there are actually two courses at Kempton — The Jubilee Course and the Round Course. There is yet another for the five and six furlong races. On the round course I believe the top-weights may have an advantage. The Jubilee Course, apart from the turn into the straight can be qoite a gallop.

Kempton is perfectly flat and suitable for most animals although, as I say, the turn into the straight is tight.

On Bank Holidays the train from Waterloo is the best bet for Kempton. There is a special station just beside the paddock. If coming by car on a public holiday you must always take into account that in the same area there are hundreds of visitors at nearby Hampton Court and the large fair which sometimes sets up beside it. Also worth noting is that some of the roads around Kempton are vital links to Heathrow Airport.

ITV have taken over viewing rights at Kempton recently.

Draw The draw is of little importance.

Leicester: Group Three: Right-Handed

The thing that struck me the first time I saw Leicester racecourse was the severe hill in the straight. It is a rigorous task for a horse in the closing stages of a race. If you are going to have a plunge on an animal at Leicester make sure it can get the distance. If it is soft, tread very carefully. I don't think there is any advantage for us with our top-weights there. The run-in is about four and a half furlongs. There is a straight mile also — downhill for about four furlongs — which joins the previously mentioned uphill climb. The course is quite a gallop, being one and three quarter miles round.

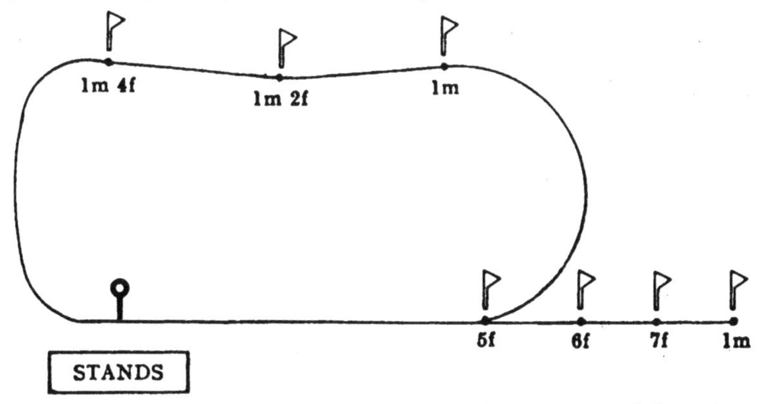

The track is two miles from the centre of Leicester and there is a good bus service. I sometimes go up there by the fast Inter-City trains. I like Leicester itself although one night I got thrown out of a club there for trying to chat up a young lady beside me at the bar. How the hell was I supposed to know she was the bouncer's girlfriend?

Draw Nothing in it at Leicester.

Lingfield: Group Two: Left-Handed

It used to be said that the sun never set on the British Empire. Well, in my mind, the sun never sets on Lingfield Park. Sure they have their foul days down there, but any time I think of the place I immediately conjure up a picture of a country pub lunch, an afternoon of glorious sunshine among the Lingfield trees, and a pleasant evening's drinking in the village at night. In summer the sun seems to shine there endlessly.

It is easy to drive down to Lingfield from London. It is only about twenty five miles from the capital. There is also a good train service from Victoria and a covered walk from the station to the course.

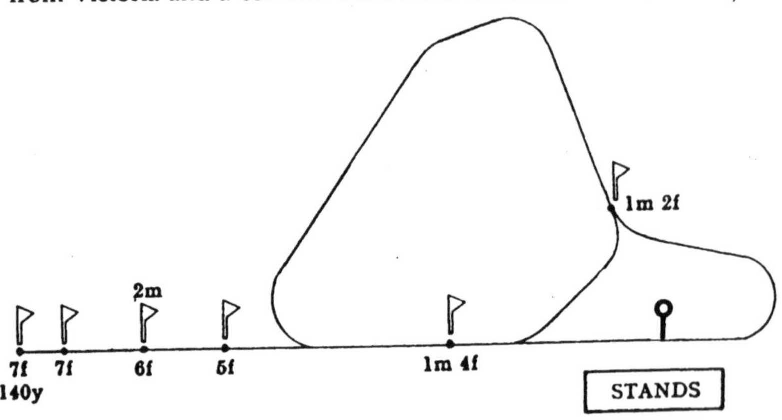

Lingfield is similar in structure to Epsom, the hill and turn into the straight resembling Tattenham Corner closely. Naturally the points in favour for us at Epsom apply to Lingfield, although sometimes on the round course handicaps, the standard of horse is not quite as good as at the Group One track. The straight seven furlong course is downhill until about three furlongs from home and then practically level up to the winning post. This is a really fast course, especially on firm ground.

The course in general is easy and the short three furlong run-in suits our plans admirably.

I would recommend Lingfield to anyone for a day out. The place was taken over by Ladbrokes recently and, although the idea was abhorent to me at first, I now concede that they have generated much new interest there and improved the place considerably.

Draw The advantage in the draw on the straight course seems to vary with the going. High numbers are best on good ground, while low numbers are favoured when it's heavy. On the round course there is no advantage.

Newbury: Group One: Left-Handed

Getting down to Newbury from London is a really smooth operation. Special express trains are laid on from Paddington and you are down in Berkshire in just under an hour. The train leaves you at the racecourse station, right outside the paddock. Naturally the course is very popular with Londoners as well as locals. In both summer and winter large crowds turn out for the Newbury meetings. The standard of racing is excellent and for many of the Berkshire trainers it is a local track. More than a few good animals are introduced to racing at the course.

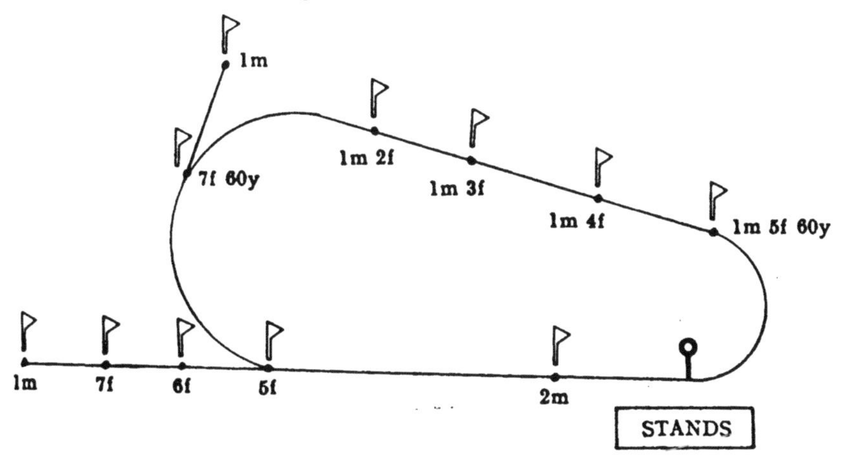

The track, with its long sweeping straight, suits all types of horses. The top-weights here really have to be able to carry their weight if they are to win. For a good accelerating animal though, there is plenty of time and room for a late challenge, although occasionally on the straight mile the horses tend to hang in a bit towards the stand's rails.

The town of Newbury is a pleasant busy little place with many small town country-style pubs. I rarely stay on there though because of the convenient special trains which leave half an hour after the last race. You are back up in London in no time.

Draw The draw has little advantage at Newbury.

Newcastle: Group One: Left-Handed

As a people, I think the Geordies are a great bunch although sometimes I can't understand a word they're saying. I suppose that's a real cheek coming from a Glaswegian, but often when I'm up there, I feel as if I'm in a foreign country. One thing I really appreciate though is the care and concern the Geordies have for a good evening's drinking — very much people after my own heart. I have friends near Whitley Bay and after a racing day I always journey through to the seaside town for some lively 'working men's club' entertainment. I quite enjoy the occasional stripper now and then.

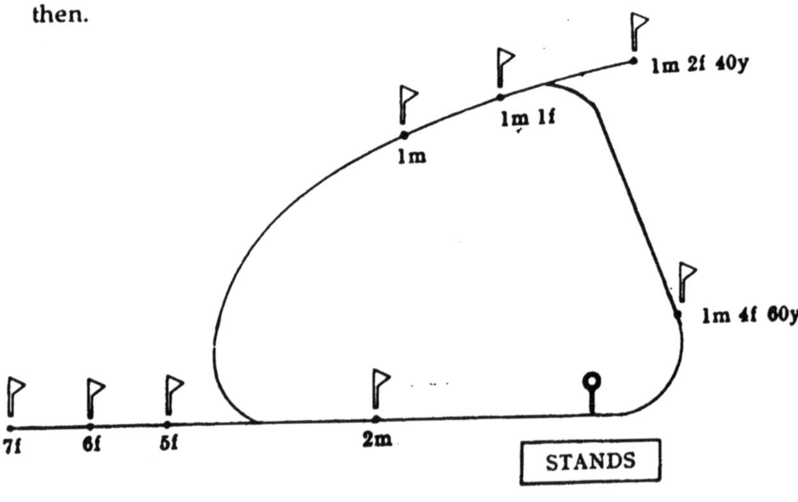

The course is nearly five miles outside the city and I always try to have the car with me up there. The amenities at Newcastle are excellent and large crowds are common, even during the winter for National Hunt Racing (the jumps). The round course is one and three quarter miles in circumference and there is also a straight seven furlongs. Both courses are stiff owing to the gradual rise throughout the four furlong run-in. Make sure that any horse you go for at Newcastle gets the distance well.

Draw The draw is unimportant.

Newmarket: Group One: Right-Handed

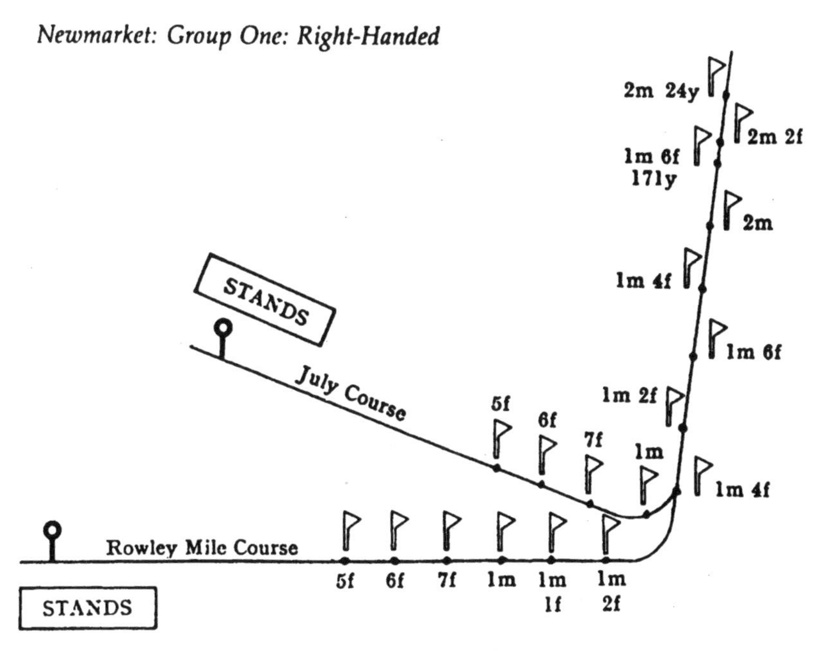

As you can see from the diagram there are two courses at Newmarket, the Rowley Mile Course and the July Course, each sharing the same stretch out in the country. On this long stretch the Cesarewitch (2m. 2f.) is run and when this and other long distance races take place, the public see very little until the horses enter their respective straights. On the Rowley Mile course there is a straight ten furlongs which, as I have said before, is a different proposition entirely to some of the turning tracks. As with Newbury, the horses allotted big weights really have to be able to carry it on this great expanse of land. Before I back a horse at Newmarket I like it to have won over a similar tough gallop. There are a few undulations at Newmarket, notably at the dip on the Rowley Mile. However, I doubt if they ever inconvenience a horse. As you would expect, Newmarket trainers plan many of their manoeuvres for the home track and this has to be borne in mind constantly.

The Rowley Mile Racecourse is centred like a mirage on a massive desert of rolling grassland with the July course just in the background. Racehorse training has been going on there for centuries and the whole place is steeped in Turf history. Needless to say, the wide expanses take a severe toll on the shoe-leather and a car is advisable for all the coming and going that Newmarket requires, such as early morning observations on the Heath, and racing a few hours later. There is a camping site at the side of the Rowley Mile Course if you fancy the outdoor life.

Newmarket is quite an undertaking just for a day out and I frequently book an hotel for a couple of nights either in the town itself or in nearby Cambridge. During university term time Cambridge is a lively spot and I have made a few friends there. I've been to some, shall we say, singular parties in the town and on one occasion found myself inside the university grounds wearing a MacGregor tartan kilt and a horned Viking helmet. A night-watchman chased me for my life. I regularly put my experiences there to good use though:

"Ever been to university old chap?"
"Yes of course."
"Where?"
"Cambridge."
"How'd it go?"
"Had to leave in a bit of a hurry I'm afraid."
"Sent down?"
"You could say that."
"Same here old boy — waiter! two large gins."

The ITV do a fully comprehensive coverage of Newmarket throughout the season.

Draw No advantage.

Nottingham: Group Three: Left-Handed

The old Robin Hood legend is played up to the hilt in Nottingham. Many of the pubs and restaurants there use the folk hero as a theme for decor. It is all very noble of course — robbing the rich to pay the poor. Something like my own philosophy — beating the bookies to pay myself.

There is one place I always like to visit when in Nottingham. It claims to be the oldest pub in England. 'Trip to Jerusalem' it is called, and is hewn out of the rock just below the castle. A cave-like little place full of charm. I've had many a little 'trip' there myself.

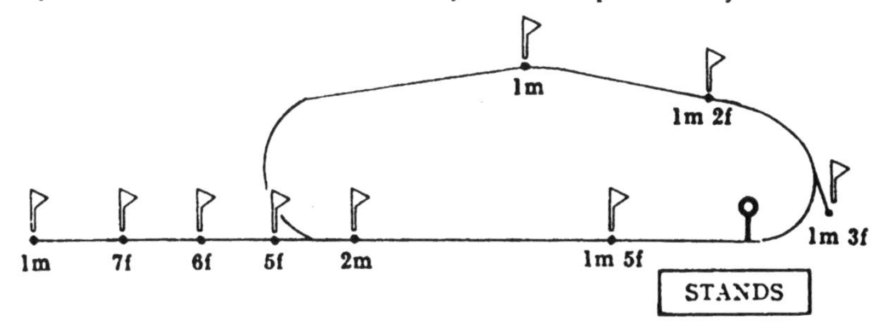

Nottingham is an easy course of about one and a half miles. The run-in is four and a half furlongs in length. There used to be a straight mile although only five and six furlong races take place on it now. The long straight ensures that every horse has an equal chance, and there is little advantage for our weight-carriers.

Draw There is not much in it although high numbers are said to have a slight advantage on the straight course.

Pontefract: Group Three: Left-Handed

Pontefract is one of those courses which is hard to define precisely. Although there are tight bends and undulations, the track is quite tough due to the last three furlongs being uphill. On soft ground it can be a severe haul and in general jockeyship often wins the day here. On firmish ground our top-weights may have a slight advantage but on soft they do not.

The town, like Doncaster, is in the heart of mining territory and although the place still maintains a certain amount of charm, industry tends to dominate the area.

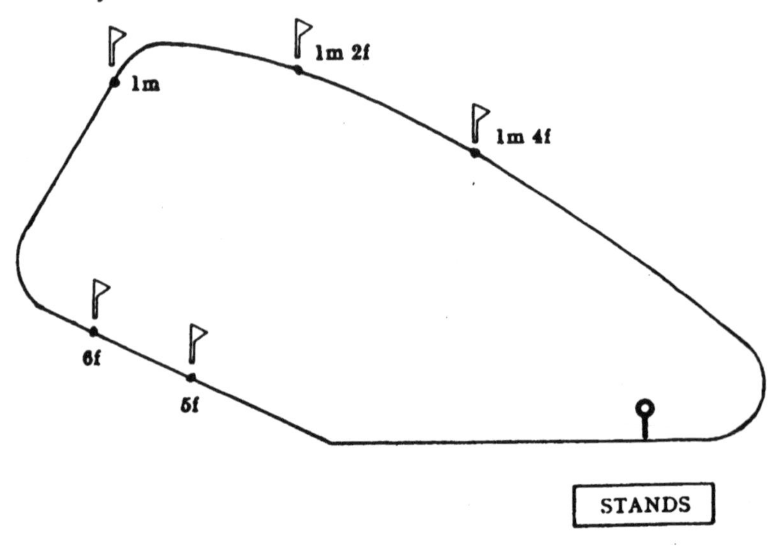

Draw **Because of the dog-leg in the straight low numbers are best in the sprints. Speed from the stalls is essential if a horse is not going to be crowded out.**

Redcar: Group Two: Left-Handed

The Redcar track is perfectly flat and just over one and three quarter miles round. There is a straight nine furlongs on which all the sprints are run. Although the track is quite narrow, the horses normally set up a good gallop, particularly on the straight course. Weight-carriers have no advantage. Apart from the sharp bend into the straight, the course could not be said to be a difficult one.

The facilities and general maintenance of Redcar offer the racegoer a very pleasant day's sport. I could easily see it becoming a

Group One course one day. It is essentially a holiday meeting with large crowds a regular feature. The town is an old fishing village

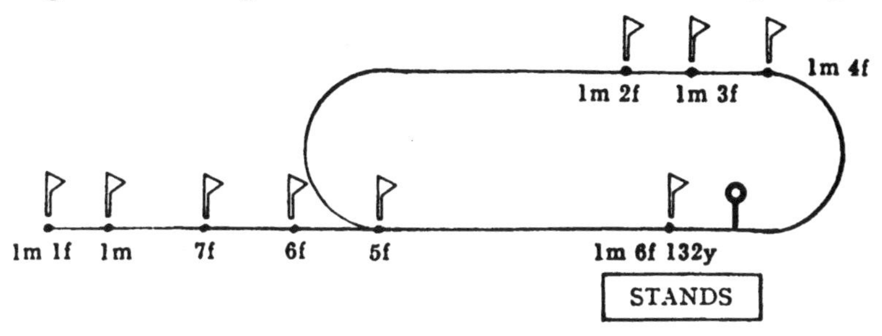

with holidaymaking taking precedence over everything else nowadays. The beach is excellent if you are a sand lover and apparently, at one time, the racing took place there.

A Glasgow couple I know live in Redcar and I'm always well looked after up there. The girl used to be an old flame of mine and I still fancy her quite a bit. But I'll say right now that, even although that bloke does regular nightshift, I would never lay a hand on her — I swear it — swear it!

Draw The draw seems to be unimportant at Redcar — I swear it.

Ripon: Group Two: Right-Handed

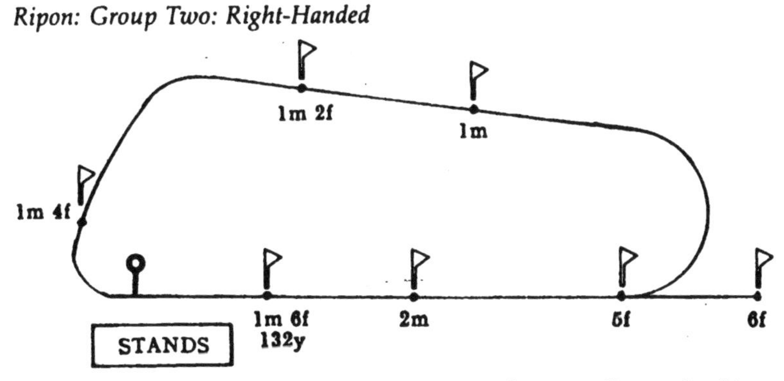

Ripon is a picturesque little city but again a bit too religious looking for me. I'll never understand Yorkshire, full of churches and racecourses. Must be some kind of plan in there somewhere. Of course I've known a few holy men who like their gambling and drinking. Takes their minds off women I fancy. Personally I'm not averse to the lot — gambling, drinking, and women.

The course is quite near the centre of town and is just short of one and three quarter miles in circumference. There is a dead straight six furlong course. The bends at Ripon are a shade tight and there are undulations in the long five furlong run-in. There is no particular advantage to any type of horses there, however, the bumpy straight could well hinder out and out gallopers.

Many of the trainers based at nearby Malton make successful raids to both Thirsk and Ripon.

Draw There is not much in it at Ripon.

Salisbury: Group Two: Right & Left-Handed

Like Lingfield, Salisbury racecourse is a very pleasant place to be on a warm summer's day. High up on the plains just outside town it offers ample respite for anyone wishing to get away from it all and escape the rigours of city life. The place is very picturesque and I thoroughly enjoy a couple of days down at the Wiltshire track. A fast train from Waterloo gets you there in just over an hour and a half and there is a bus service from the railway station up into the country.

The track is quite a stiff one, being uphill for the final four furlongs. There is a loop at the far end of the course and, in the long

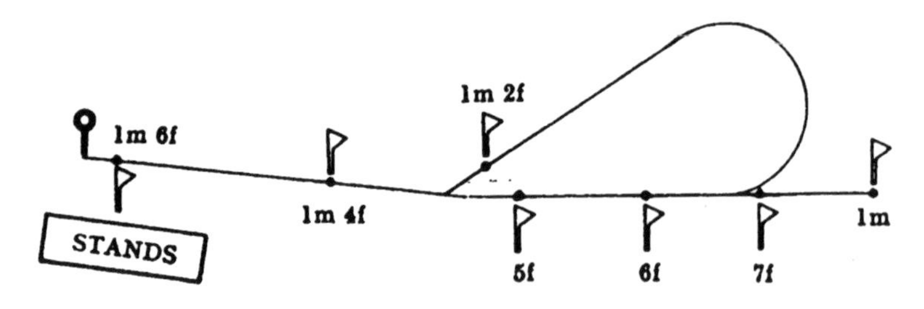

distance races, the horses gallop away from the stands to start with and then come back up the straight to finish. Although the loop is quite sharp, the tough uphill four furlong straight cancels out any top-weight advantage there.

Salisbury itself is a quaint historical town with many interesting buildings. I've spent a few evenings there and found the cider excellent in numerous establishments. If you are a really keen outdoor type you can always visit nearby Stonehenge. From personal experience though, don't try it around midnight.

Draw High numbers are slightly favoured on the straight course.

Sandown: Group One: Right Handed

In nearly all racing publications Sandown Park is portrayed as a stiff galloping track. On the round course I do not agree with this at all. For one thing, the bend round into the straight is pretty tight and few jockeys allow their mounts to go flat out down the back stretch knowing this sharp bend is coming up. I think, in spite of all that has been written, the top-weights have a big advantage at Sandown and I have backed many a long-priced winner following this belief. Another factor to be taken into account is: the standard of horse running in the Sandown handicaps is usually high, and a good jockey can bide his time until the straight before delivering a late challenge. Consequently, Sandown is the ideal place for a horse with a good turn of foot.

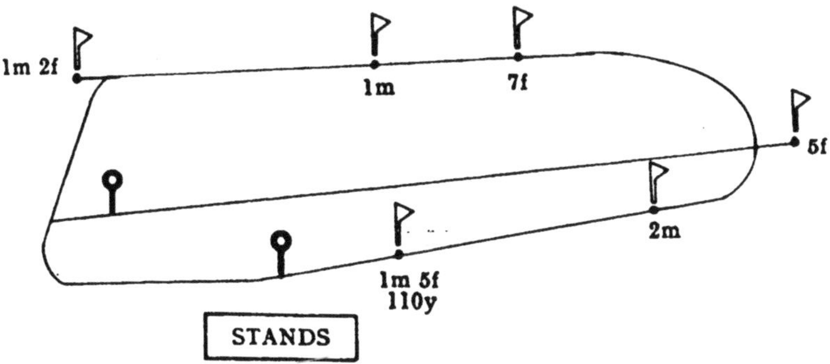

There is a separate five furlong course and this definitely is stiff, being uphill all the way.

Sandown is the nearest racecourse to my home. It takes me about half an hour to get down to Esher where the track is situated. To live in Esher you have to start thinking in stockbroker terms. The whole area is very flash. Being only fifteen miles or so from London (Waterloo-Esher), Sandown never fails to attract a good crowd. Proximity aside, the course is one of the best in the country, the amenities, viewing, and racing, being second to none. The course is very popular with all the top trainers.

Many Londoners take their families to Sandown and in the middle of the track there is a swing park for the children. Unfortunately, on the rare occasion I had my son along, he brought all the escalating stairs to a halt.

Draw On the round course there is little advantage. On the five stretch low numbers are said to be best.

Stockton (Teeside): Group Four: Left-Handed

Stockton changed its name to Teeside in 1967 and then recently changed it back to Stockton again. Then, in July 1981, it was announced the course would close . . . so the name changes obviously did not help very much.

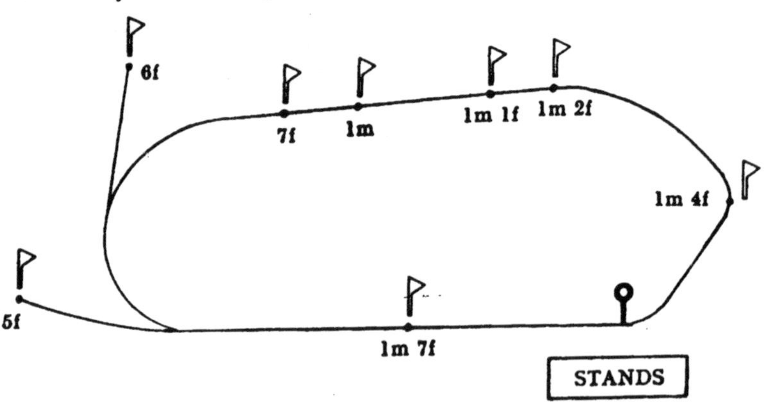

For the record, the course was nearly one and three quarter miles round and a bit sharp. The run-in was four furlongs in length. There were separate shoots for the starts of the five and six furlong races.

Any time I went up there I always felt duty bound to visit my friends in Redcar, being so near and all — I swear it.

Draw Low numbers were best in sprints.

Thirsk: Group Two: Left-Handed

Thirsk is a very popular little Yorkshire track and trainers from the nearby Malton training area frequently lay out horses to win there The course is only one and a quarter miles round and obviously on the sharp side. There is a straight, slightly undulating, six furlong course for the sprints. It is well worth while keeping an eye on the top-weights on any course one and a quarter miles round although at Thirsk, the four furlong straight and slightly uphill finish can counter the advantage somewhat.

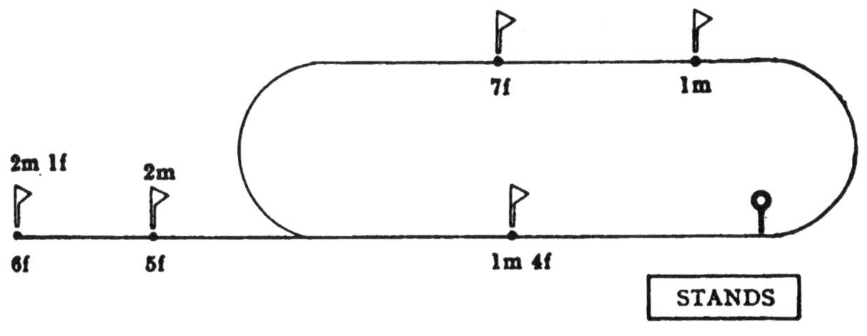

Thirsk itself is an old-fashioned market town and there is absolutely no excuse for being thirsty there. I've never known a town with so many little inns. A fascinating spot for an evening's activity. The people are extremely friendly too.

Draw High numbers seem to have an advantage on the straight course.

Warwick: Group Four: Left-Handed

Although there are tight bends at Warwick there is plenty of room on the track. It is very wide indeed. You would expect, with the sharp bends and short two and a half furlong run-in, that top-weights would be in an advantageous position, however, in the long back stretch, where the six and seven furlong starts are situated, the horses set up a good strong gallop, making jockeyship, especially pace-judgement, an important factor at the track. All-out gallopers really get going on this back straight but the sharp home turn puts paid to many of them. There is a separate course for the five furlong races.

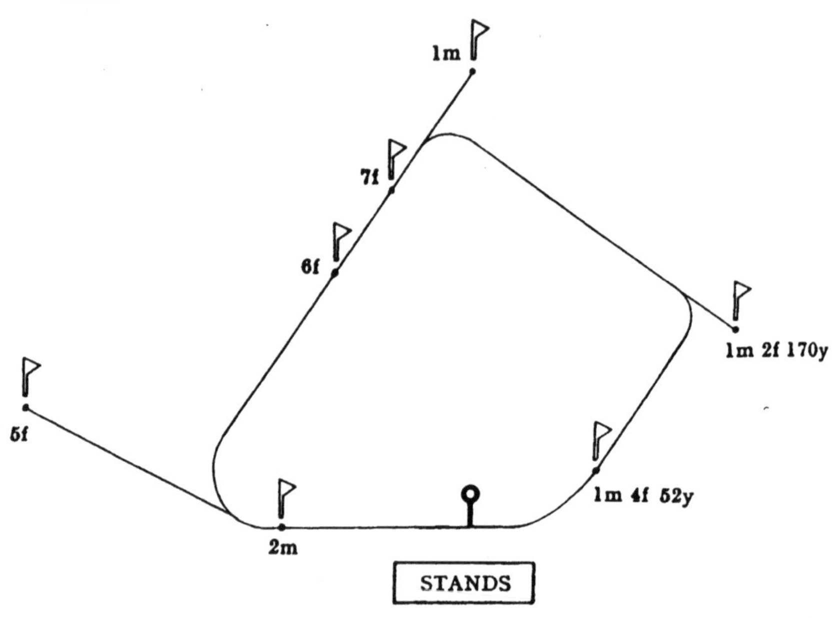

Warwick is a fair old place to find yourself for a drink but the castle there put me quite ill at ease with the locals. The torture chamber frightened the life out of me — so devilishly cunning it was. I must admit right enough, the young companion who was with me during my visit showed great enthusiasm for the place — especially the whips, chains, and leather gear. I had a hell of a job getting her out to go for a drink

Draw Because of the tight bend into the short straight, low numbers have a big advantage there in races up to a mile.

Windsor: Group Three: Right & Left-Handed

Windsor is a rather unusual course being in the shape of a figure eight. The only other similar track I know is the National Hunt course at Fontwell Park down near Goodwood. Although the bends are tight, the last six furlongs is straight, apart from one dog-leg, and the horses can really get going on this part of the track. The handicaps there are not of the highest calibre and unless you are interested in a horse with definite quickening powers, then it pays to tread warily. Windsor also stages many sprint races and, quite frankly, I do not go there too often. The Windsor executive go in for regular night meetings, on Mondays mainly, with the occasional Saturday fixture. Great crowds turn out for them from the surrounding area and London.

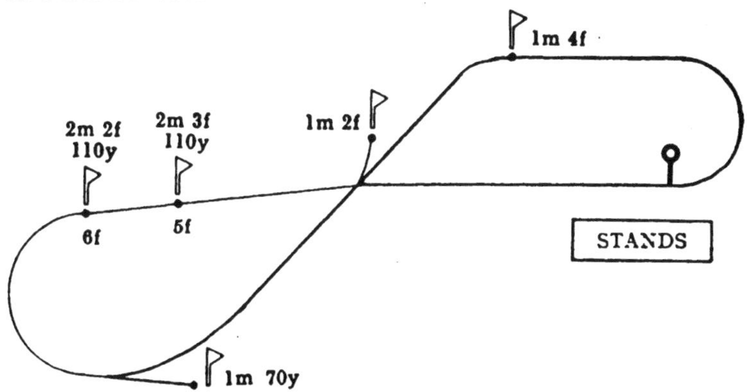

Windsor is a tourist centre with the Castle and boating on the Thames the main attractions. There are some lovely little pubs in the town centre and around the river, and a novel addition to racing is the boat trip from Windsor Railway Station to the track which lies on the banks of the river.

Draw In the sprint races high numbers are best.

Wolverhampton: Group Four: Left-Handed

Wolverhampton is slightly more than one and a half miles round and flat throughout. The run-in is five furlongs long and quite a gallop. There is also a straight five furlong course which, because of the flat ground, can be very fast on firmish ground. There is no weight advantage for us here and, in fact, big plodding gallopers can really start motoring on the long straight — at Group Four level, a tricky proposition for backers.

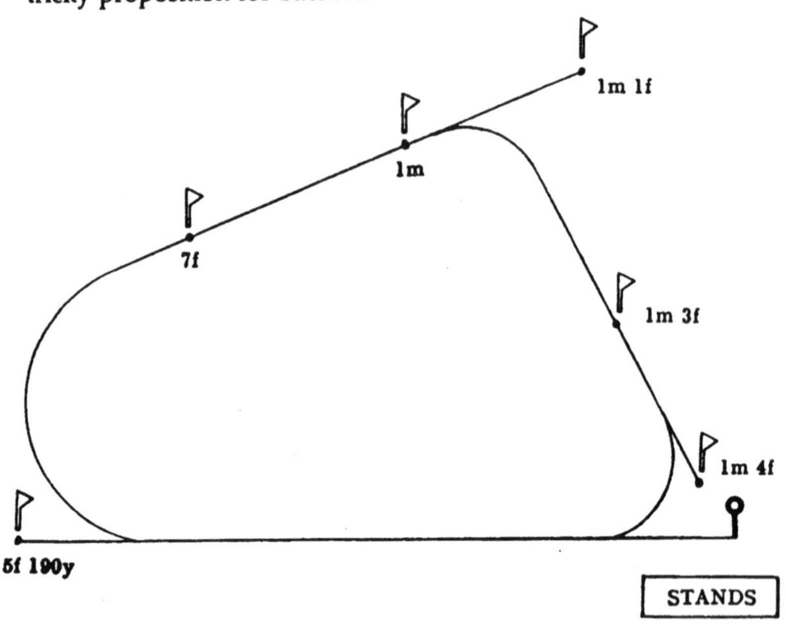

The amenities at Wolverhampton are good and although some of the handicaps are of pretty low calibre, they can be watched in comfort.

Draw There is not much in it here.

Yarmouth: Group Three: Left-Handed

The racecourse at Great Yarmouth is near the centre of town and during the holiday months the place gets packed out. For many Newmarket trainers Yarmouth is a home from home and some days the majority of winners are Newmarket trained. The track is one mile five furlongs round and rather narrow, but it could not be said that it was sharp, owing to the long flat five furlong straight. There is also a straight mile and on firm ground the horses are really flying by the time they reach the winning post. No weight advantage here I'm afraid.

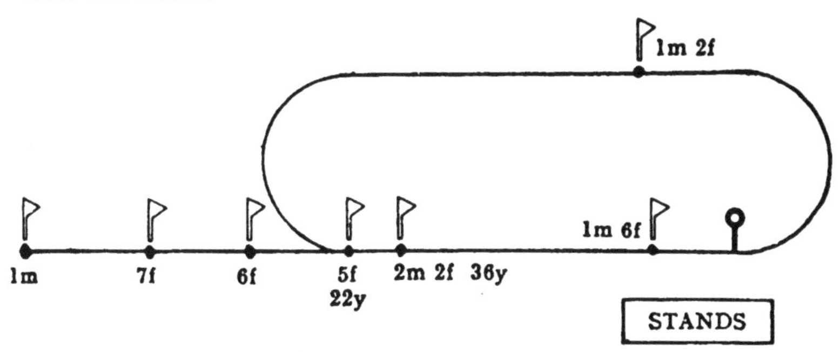

The town itself has all the fun of the fair you would expect at a seaside holiday resort. I've gone camping up that way occasionally and taken in race meetings while on holiday. I nearly had the law on me once for making a book at one of the holiday camps.

Draw No advantage.

York: Group One: Left-Handed

York is a tremendous racecourse. Everything about it is the best, including the stands, the amenities, the racing, and even the flowers and trees. It is a really beautiful course and a must for anyone who wishes to watch the sport in style. There has been horse racing in Yorkshire for as long as anyone can remember and, in fact, throughout the shire, there are no less than eight Flat racecourses. The Yorkshire people certainly enjoy their racing and friends I have up there do their own 'Yorkshire circuit' in the same way as I comb the 'London' tracks.

I must admit right now that the chapters in this book lean heavily towards South of England racing. Naturally you must, to start with anyway, work out a little circuit for yourself. Many good horses start their racing careers in the North and if you are lucky enough to spot one, as I did with Tesoro Mio at Ayr, then often you are way ahead of the pack, and good prices can be had in subsequent races, before the Southern Press boys latch on.

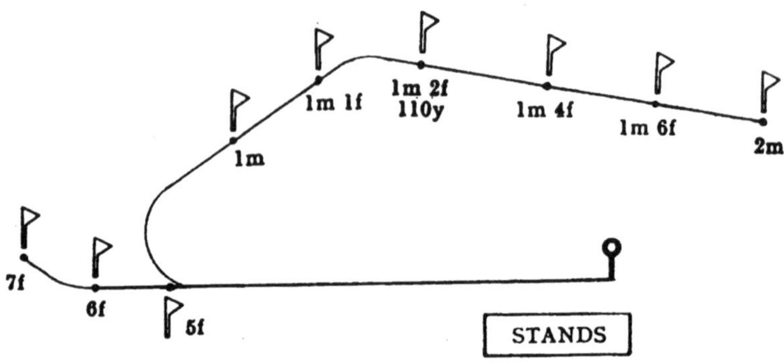

The track at York is flat with wide easy bends. No particular type of horse is favoured here and the long straight rules out a definite top-weight advantage. Some good top-weights win there though because of the high standard of racing and better class handicappers. One of the most important races at York, as far as we are concerned, is the John Smith's Magnet Cup run over one mile, two and a half furlongs in July. I have often backed the winner of this race.

If you fancy yourself as a bit of an historian then York is the place for you. The city is steeped in history stretching right back to Roman times. I have spent many an hour just wandering through York in a kind of architectural pub-crawl. I remember late one night thinking I had come across a new wonder of the world — the leaning towers of York Minster.

Draw High numbers are favoured in the sprint races, more so on soft ground.

Irish Racing

Although I have been to a few race meetings in Ireland over the years, in no way could I ever consider it my 'patch'. As I mentioned earlier in this book, it is the extremely difficult task of pulling

French, Irish, and British form together that has made me work out my plans to cover only racing which is easily accessible to me. For example, if you live in the North and wish to start your campaign at the Scottish and Northern English tracks, then it is a bit foolish of me recommending keeping an eye on the top-weights at Tralee in the South West of Ireland. But quite naturally, if you live in that part of Ireland, then the little circuit of courses in your area is of paramount importance.

Knowing how closely and fanatically the Irish public study British racing, I feel duty bound to include a few words about the Irish courses in this work although I will not attempt the same detail as I have with the British ones, some of which are literally second homes to me.

The Irish do not grade their tracks as in Britain e.g. Ascot (Grade One) Lingfield (Grade Two). However, it is recognised that the tracks of the 'Dublin Circuit' offer the higher class racing. In particular, you could regard The Curragh, Leopardstown, and Phoenix Park, as equivalent to British Grade One tracks.

Below I have made a list of the Irish tracks along with some *personal* comments about them, bearing in mind that with racing anywhere in the world, a good accelerating horse, once you've spotted it, has a much easier task when it is allotted top weight and is racing against inferior opposition at a tight turning racecourse. But again, *and especially in rainy Ireland*, beware of the soft ground when putting money on flat racing.

Ballinrobe	(R.H.) (Right-handed): A very sharp track. Always consider the handicap top-weights.
Bellewstown	(L.H.) Sharp. Note the top-weights.
Clonmel	(R.H.) A good gallop this one. Doubly check your selection's stamina here.
The Curragh	(R.H.) A severe galloping track. Staying power essential.
Downpatrick	(R.H.) Sharp, but a bit of a climb to the winning post.
Down Royal	(R.H.) A galloping course suiting the big plodders.

Dundalk	(L.H.) A bit sharp and tricky. A good jockey is worth a couple of lengths here.
Fairyhouse	(R.H.) A galloping track.
Galway	(R.H.) Quite a gallop. Make sure your horse gets the distance.
Gowran Park	(R.H.) Rather galloping in nature.
Killarney	(L.H.) Sharp and a bit tricky. Watch the top-weights.
Kilbeggan	(R.H.) Again sharp and tricky. Top-weights.
Laytown Strand	Racing takes place on the beach. A unique day's racing.
Leopardstown	(L.H.) Definitely a galloping track. Top-weights have quite a task here.
Limerick	(R.H.) Sharpish, but really heavy in bad weather.
Limerick Junction	(L.H.) An average-type level course which does not really throw up any advantages or disadvantages.
Listowel	(L.H.) Very sharp. Consider your top-weights here although only on good ground. A bit of a mud bath after heavy rain.
Mallow	(R.H.) A galloping track with little advantage to our top-weights.
Naas	(L.H.) Definitely galloping in nature. Staying power essential here.
Navan	(L.H.) Again a hell of a gallop. Big plodding stayers can gallop their rivals into the ground here.
Phoenix Park	(L. & R.H.) Galloping again, especially up the home stretches.
Punchestown	(R.H.) Another galloping track.
Roscommon	(R.H.) Sharp in places but rather tough owing to the uphill finish.
Sligo	(R.H.) Sharp. Watch the top-weights here.

Thurles	(R.H.) Sharp and rather hilly. Jockeyship important here.
Tralee	(R.H.) Sharp and small. Good top-weights have a decided advantage here.
Tramore	(R.H.) Very sharp and extremely tricky. Again watch the top-weights but an experienced jockey is a good idea too.
Wexford	(R.H.) Sharp. Watch the top of the handicap.

I haven't been to Ireland for some time now. I'll never forget that last day I was there. Shannon Airport it was. Those two detectives have stuck in my memory all these years.

"We know it was only a wee harmless party Mister Simpson but things are just a little bit different here than in London."

"But officer, those lassies were convent girls with a good Catholic upbringing."

"We still think it would be a good idea if you didn't come back!"

CHAPTER 6

Jockeyship

Many people who back racehorses use ratings on which to base their selections. That is to say, they either rate the horses themselves, use the ratings in their daily newspaper, or purchase ratings from the organisations who specialise in such work. Always remember though, that any ratings you see for handicaps are only an alternative opinion of the merits of horses, as opposed to the opinion of the official handicappers who, as I have mentioned before, weight all the horses to finish at the winning post in a theoretical multiple photo-finish. When you hear someone saying that a horse is 'well in at the weights' all this means is, one of the big organisations such as Timeform or Raceform has a higher regard for a certain animal than racing officialdom. Often they are proved right. The official handicappers are not infallible, although I personally have the highest regard for them.

You may be wondering why I've started off a chapter on jockeyship with a paragraph on racehorse ratings. The thing is, I believe that jockeyship, or the lack of it, can make a complete nonsense of ratings, especially on tracks that require a bit of riding such as Epsom or Chester. One of the leading racing literature organisations suggests that when using their ratings, you may add a point or two (pound or two) on to the rating of a horse with an outstanding jockey aboard. I believe this to be a gross understatement and forward the theory that a top flight jockey can make as much as half a stone difference (7 lbs. approx. 2 lengths) to a horse. Bear in mind always that jockeyship is of paramount importance on the Turf, in spite of all the ratings and mathematical calculations.

You will notice, of course, that every jockey at some time or another has his day. Even the 'bad' jocks will occasionally notch up a winner or two. This happens a lot at the minor meetings where few of the horses have the qualities we are seeking. At a meeting full of one-paced plodders anything can happen.

Don't get me wrong by the way, the top men are not always dead certs even if a horse has all the form, finishing speed, and breeding going for it. Jockeys can all make mistakes — and frequently do. But you must consider the question in the same light as staking out your money for betting. It must again be an exercise evaluated 'in the long run', and in the long term it is far more profitable backing the top jockeys who ride the most winners.

I've often thought that if it weren't for racing we would never, in a million years, pay the slightest attention to these funny little men unless they appeared covered in paint at the local circus. But because of the vast amounts of money involved in breeding, betting, and prizes, these freaky little fellows are projected into figures of national importance. In various racing publications, and on TV, journalists and broadcasters drool and dribble over jockeys as if they are some phenomenon from another planet. At the track you will see, even the most prestigious celebrities, toadying and crawling at the very sight of Lester, Willie, or Pat. Why they do it I'll never know. In all the newspaper articles and television interviews I've ever seen, I've never known a jockey to say anything of importance in relation to future winner-finding. They are surpassed only by politicians in the art of talking and saying absolutely nothing. If you yourself try to say a few words to a jockey at a race meeting, you will be shunned as if you have a bad attack of leprosy.

Personally I have little time for any of them except in their official capacity as race-riders.

This may sound callous and mercenary but from what I have seen and heard over many years on the Turf, jockeys themselves, trainers, bookies, and backers, are all involved in racing for one thing and one thing only — money!

Owners too of course, but with them sometimes swank and self-esteem take precedence over financial matters.

With the above in mind then and without, I hope, any sickly back-scratching, I will present a list of jockeys who, I think, can give a horse a good chance of winning. You must always remember though, that occasionally a small stable will come up with a real good accelerating animal and use their regular jockey for the horse in its races. Then of course, the jock may not be one of the very top men. I am afraid this is the kind of situation where your own judgement must be used. I am not prepared to say here who I think are bad jockeys but perhaps my section on a typical season (see page 129) will offer you guidance here.

In this chapter I am only including the jockeys who, in my reckoning, are outstanding, and give a horse an actual advantage.

Willie Carson Willie's main asset is his strength. Once he gets in front with an animal in the straight, it is one hell of a job catching him. He is first class in a finish and gives his all when riding. Of course the main thing Willie has going for him at the moment is his stable — that of Dick Hern. There is a load of money behind that outfit. In the years to come I think the present day combination of Hern/Carson will be looked upon as legendary in Turf history. Without taking anything away from Willie, I believe that some of the horses Dick Hern turns out only have to be pointed in the right direction to win.

Pat Eddery Pat, like Willie Carson, is really strong in a finish but what I like about his riding is his positional sense. He is a master at weaving through a big field and getting into a good challenging position. He rarely gets boxed in or out. An excellent rider now with the back up of the powerful Vincent O'Brien/Robert Sangster outfit in Ireland. Pat won the 1980 Arc de Triumph on Detroit soon after joining this team and many more famous victories can be expected in the coming years.

Eddie Hide Edward's knowledge and judgement of the Northern racecourses is unequalled and I believe he is a big advantage to a horse up there. He rides frequently in the South nowadays but undoubtedly the North is his métier.

Joe Mercer Many racing enthusiasts were shocked when Joe was replaced by Willie Carson as first jockey to Dick Hern a few years ago. However, his subsequent move to Henry Cecil proved a blessing in disguise. Last year (1979), for the first time in his long career, he became champion jockey with 164 winners from 608 rides. That is a percentage of 26.97% — slightly over one winner in every four rides.

Say no more!

Joe moves to Peter Walwyn's Lambourn stable following the departure of Pat Eddery to Ireland.

Lester Piggott So much has been written about Lester Piggott that little I can say here will make an impression on anybody. For our purposes though, Lester is the ideal jockey for our good top-weighted animals. His judgement and positioning are excellent. He knows just when to produce a horse in distance handicap races and I don't know how many times I've seen him doing it to perfection with just a head or a neck to spare. This is far more important than people think, and not just for the sake of being slick or clever. If a good accelerating handicapper can keep winning by the narrowest of margins, then the handicappers can only re-assess it accordingly, leaving the horse plenty in hand for the future.

The excellent handicapper House Guard illustrates this point well. In the seasons 1978 and 1979 Piggott won no less than eight handicaps on House Guard. Take note of the distances he won by on each of these occasions:

Neck	¾ length
1 length	Short Head
Head	½ length
¾ length	Neck

An amazing piece of riding.

John Reid Many of our top jockeys have been at the game for years. Willie Carson was a long time in reaching the top and spent many a season plodding away until the present-day big time arrived.

I believe John Reid will become a great jockey one day. He seems to be a young man who knows exactly where he's going and in a quiet systematic way is gaining experience all the time. He is only young yet but has all the attributes necessary to last for years. He is strong, cool, and a good judge of a race. On one occasion I saw him out alone before racing at Epsom, studying every blade of grass in the most dedicated fashion — definitely a young chap to keep an eye on.

Already John has made the history books with his efforts on Ile de Bourbon, one of the best horses of recent years.

Greville Starkey Greville is another who is very powerful in a finish. He frequently appears late on the scene in his races and is an excellent judge of a horse's quickening powers.

1978 was definitely Greville's year when, as well as many other fine victories, he won the Derby on Shirley Heights and the Oaks on Fair Salina.

CHAPTER 7

Trainers

As with jockeys, it is a good idea to rely on trainers who have a proven track record and know what they are about in terms of placing their horses in handicaps. Unlike jockeys, however, trainers are stuck with the horses they have in their yards at any given time and cannot study the form books and pick and choose whatever animals they would like to be involved with.

Subsequently, many skilful trainers go through lean patches simply because the horses they acquire are not good enough to win many races. It is difficult, therefore, to decide just who are good and who are bad trainers. If a horse arrives on the scene with the attributes we are seeking then even the most moderate of yards can prepare it and turn it out to win good races.

This of course is all swings and roundabouts talk and like everything else in racing, money often determines the success of stables. Year after year statistics show that some trainers invariably turn out more winners than their rivals. Naturally the big powerful stables with plenty of money behind them are in the most advantageous position in this respect, if only by the force of numbers of horses they run.

Personally I am in no way convinced that all these huge stables are the most skilful — far from it. I believe there is only a handful of people in racehorse training who really know what they are doing. The others, like some of our big personality football managers, seem far better talking about the sport than actually producing the goods. How some of the 'big' trainers got into their elevated positions, I'll never know. Perhaps racehorse training is more about public relations than talent.

Anyway, I have again set out some of my favourite trainers for you. The list is not rigid by any means and you are perfectly entitled to form your own opinion of trainers no matter how big or small. As you will see, my list tends to centre around Southern racing.

Henry Cecil Henry never makes any secret of what he believes a horse's abilities are. I suppose nowadays though, with bookies' communications so good, it is foolish to try the big undercover games at a place such as Newmarket Heath which has more 'spies' per square yard than Berlin. Nevertheless, if you ask Henry Cecil about the chances of one of his runners, he'll tell you quite openly and honestly. An admirable chap who's good and knows it. Like myself, he seems to find much of the pomposity and swank of the racecourse a bit of a pain in the neck.

Lester Piggott teamed up with him for the 1981 season — a real money-making duo if ever I saw one.

Paul Cole Paul is always a man to keep an eye on in the big handicaps. He seems to have a good understanding of what is required in that field and pulls off many a good-priced winner when nobody expects it. Nobody except me of course. I can often read Paul's mind and profit regularly by doing so.

A shrewd trainer who also has the knack of turning out his horses at the track in beautiful condition.

John Dunlop After his recent success with Shirley Heights in the 1978 Derby and Quick As Lightning in the 1980 One Thousand Guineas, John is now looked to for Classic potential — and quite rightly so. However, for our purposes in handicap racing, he is indispensable and you must include him in your plan of action immediately no matter where you live — North or South.

John, with the regular assistance of Willie Carson (if available) pulls off many handicap victories each year and it is very profitable indeed following him. From what he has said on television and in newspaper quotations, it is obvious he thinks along the very same lines as myself on racecourse structure. He places his horses accordingly and, if you understand the game, it is not too difficult to predict what he's up to.

Like Henry Cecil, John is perfectly open about the chances of his horses. A thorough gentleman and handicap expert.

Guy Harwood Guy is a good man to follow around the Southern Circuit tracks such as Lingfield, Brighton, and Folkestone. With jockey Greville Starkey he wins many handicaps each year for the older horses and is quite an expert at placing them in this type of event.

Dick Hern Dick is well known for the powerful string of high class classic animals he produces each year and much of the press comment the stable receives is centred around these champions. But leaving them aside, the stable has a steady stream of good handicappers too and in placing them to win, Dick has few equals. First-time-out winners are common and at the track the stable's horses are turned out quite magnificently with that lovely rich sheen that indicates an animal ready to run for its life.

I have the highest regard for Dick Hern although he prefers to keep very much to himself and his rich and Royal owners. Recently he has been criticised for not offering enough information to the media. For my money, the results he gets with his horses speak for themselves.

Ryan Price Ryan is another master at turning out horses in peak condition at the track. His horses are always fit to run at their best and the stable has a go at everything from 'maidens' right through to top class Group One events.

Ryan is a shrewd character who understands just how to place a horse to the best advantage, although when things don't go his way, he makes no bones or spares no language letting the world know about it. A rather tempestuous individual who is better admired from afar.

I'm damned if I'd like to work for him.

Micheal Stoute Micheal has really burst on to the scene in recent years and now commands the reputation of being one of our top trainers. He wins many handicaps and sometimes you will see one of his horses running up a sequence of wins.

A chap who seems to enjoy a good laugh.

Jeremy Tree Jeremy is a real shrewd character who operates every year with only a small string of horses. With his small team he pulls off some tremendous coups, generally in handicaps and top class races. There are never many runners from the Tree stable but when they do appear, consider them very carefully indeed.

Peter Walwyn Peter is undoubtedly one of the best trainers around at the present time although recently the stable has been plagued with virus troubles. Like Dick Hern, he is looked upon each season to come up with the country's main classic contenders. In handicaps however, he has few masters. When the new Walwyn/Joe Mercer combination appears in your morning paper it must be seriously taken account of. Peter can place his horses to win with uncanny foresight and it is a foolish man who leaves him out of the reckoning in the really top-bracket handicaps.

Peter, a pleasant but very crafty man, is a must for our plans.

As I have said earlier, this list gives only a few examples of what to look for in a trainer. Because I have not mentioned someone here does not necessarily mean I have little regard for them. Smaller outfits regularly perform magnificent training feats with individual horses. The thing is, the men I have mentioned above do it year after year and can be depended on as a basic backbone for our operation. To put it another way, if you fancy a horse in a handicap and some of the above stables have horses running against your's, tread very carefully and check out all your facts before you oppose these proven masters.

CHAPTER 8

Ten Recent Flyers

After a couple of chapters on jockeys and trainers I think it's about time we brought some horses into the picture. A natural progression you might agree, but it's amazing how many publications ignore such an intrinsic part of the racing scene. Many works are so obsessed by statistics about trainers, jockeys, and betting, that you sometimes wonder why the sport isn't changed into some electronic numbers game and the horses eliminated altogether. Don't ever forget that all those thousands of high street shops and their employees depend one hundred per cent on the horses and dogs which gallop endlessly round circuits all over Britain every week. As I have said somewhere else, it is the uncertainty of the sport which makes it such a money-spinner.

My list does not include the usual band of Derby and 'Guineas' winners: no Nijinsky's, Mill Reef's, or Troy's here I'm afraid. There are, however, ten, as I see it, exceptional handicappers — the type you should be on the look-out for to fill your notebook. This is my list of recent 'champions'.

Air Trooper: As a three-year-old Air Trooper was no more than an average handicapper, recording a couple of mid-season victories at Nottingham and Salisbury (mile handicap). He won another handicap at Ripon but was placed second after a stewards' inquiry. He had crossed the second horse in the dash for the line. Subsequently, he entered 1977 rated around 45, just high enough to sneak into the Lincoln (45+). Unfortunately he was balloted out of the big race because of the high number of entries that year. Bill Wightman, his trainer, gave him another run at the Lincoln Meeting in an Apprentice race, but the horse made no show in the really soft ground which, in my opinion, never suited him.

As I said at the beginning of this book, Air Trooper fairly burst on to the scene in the Roseberry Handicap at the Kempton Easter Meeting producing, for the first time, the electrifying surge which was to be his trade mark for the rest of the season. Anyone who saw him that day (who knew something about the game) must have realised that here was a horse pounds better than his modest 45 rating. They, and me, were dead right. He finished the season rated around the 80 mark. Here are the races he won — all in brilliant style and all handicaps:

Roseberry Handicap	(40+)	: Kempton	: 10 fur.	8/1
Newbury Spring Cup	(45+)	: Newbury	: 8 fur.	10/1
Sandown Cup	(40+)	: Sandown	: 10 fur.	5/6
Hong Kong Handicap	(40+)	: Sandown	: 10 fur.	9/2
John Smith Magnet Cup	(45+)	: York	: 10 fur. 110 y.	9/2

Air Trooper went on later in the year to run a head second in the Group Two Queen Elizabeth II Stakes at Ascot. He ran only once as a five-year-old, when tailing off in a Group race at Sandown. It was quite clear that day that something was far wrong with him. He never ran again and was retired to stud. I look forward to seeing his sons and daughters.

Hang On Elvis: This big gelding was not quite in the same class as Air Trooper but in terms of the races he was aimed at, he led the handicappers a merry dance all during 1978 (as a three-year-old). He too, had a nice little finishing burst which, at his own level, continually kept him one jump ahead of his rivals.

Hang On Elvis was only lightly raced as a two-year-old, having only three runs, the last one being in a Newmarket Selling race. He was obviously not too highly regarded and was gelded (see page 143). However under the temporary handling of Derek Kent (better known as a jump trainer), the horse won a mile maiden race first time out at Brighton. Soon afterwards he switched to Neville Callaghan's stable and the young Newmarket trainer exploited to the full the gelding's liking for the Sussex track. Hang On Elvis was invincible down at Brighton from then on. His 1978 victories were:

Race		Course	Distance	Price
Aldrington Stakes	(non-handicap)	Brighton	8 fur.	9/1
Aquarium Handicap	(0-65)	Brighton	10 fur.	12/1
Royal Handicap	(0-55)	Windsor	10 fur. 22 y.	100/30
Fitzherbert Handicap	(0-65)	Brighton	12 fur.	7/4
St. Margarets Handicap	(0-60)	Leicester	12 fur.	Ev.
Telscombe Handicap	(0-55)	Brighton	12 fur.	11/10
Saltdean Handicap	(0-65)	Brighton	10 fur.	4/5

Predictably, as soon as everyone latched on to the steady improvement Hang On Elvis was making, the prices became very prohibitive.

In 1979 he again won first time out — a 10 fur. 50 yd. Doncaster handicap (0-70) at the Lincoln Meeting at 7/2, but after this win he faded as dramatically as he had improved and has never won since. At his peak though, he clearly showed what an advantage a little finishing burst can be among modest rivals.

House Guard: You will notice later, in my 'typical season', this colt featuring regularly in my betting operation. In fact, as a money-maker you could not ask for a better servant than House Guard.

As a two-year-old he had not been too impressive. After showing promise he had been backed, on a couple of occasions, to win sprint events. However, the best he could manage was a second and a third.

At three he had a kind of 'in and out' season, seemingly preferring to win only when Lester Piggott was at the helm. Whether Robert Armstrong, Piggott's brother-in-law, trained him to win when his relative was up, or whether the horse genuinely preferred to keep things in the family, is a moot point, but when other jockeys were engaged, no 'goods' materialised. I personally 'picked up' House Guard at the 'back end' of 1978, during the latter part of his three-year-old campaign. At the Goodwood October Meeting he absolutely cruised home under top weight in a 7 furlong handicap (0-65). He then went to York and faltered a bit, finishing sixth of seven in a non-handicap event. When reverting to handicap company in a Sandown 7 furlong race (35-75), he again, after being boxed-in, showed promising quickening powers when barging his way through to win by a typical Piggot-Sandown Park-head. I decided to follow him in 1979 — with Piggott of course. It was a good idea:

Brandon Handicap	(0-70)	: Newmarket	: 7 fur.	85/40
Mortlake Handicap	(0-60)	: Kempton	: 8 fur.	5/2
Playmate Handicap	(0-60)	: Sandown	: 8 fur.	3/1
Pampisford Handicap	(0-60)	: Newmarket	: 8 fur.	5/4
Hillingdon Shirt Mirage Mile Handicap	(amateur)	: Haydock	: 8 fur. 40 y.	7/1
Cavendish Cape South African Sherry Handicap	(35+)	: Ascot	: 7 fur.	7/2

House Guard was still campaigning in 1980 and has already won two handicaps although in the first of these — the Ultramar Jubilee Handicap (45+) at Kempton — he was unfortunate enough to lose the race in the stewards' room after crossing the second horse. Apart from the swerve though, he won that race very easily and no doubt he will collect further prizes before he is retired.

Northleach: The sire Northfields is well known for passing on battling qualities to his offspring and no horse bears this out more than the John Dunlop trained Northleach. Time and time again, when everyone has come to the conclusion that the handicapper has finally caught up with him, he pulls out something extra and wins more races. Later in this book you will see how I too arrived at a similar assumption only to be proved wrong as have many before me.

I think the key to Northleach is his strong finishing speed which, when combined with guts, is a formidable weapon for any jockey to have at his disposal. A horse with this combination can never really be written off and is a constant headache to the handicappers.

Northleach will never win a Group race, but within his own sphere he is always a force to be reckoned with, especially on turning tracks. His 1979 victories were as follows:

John Hudson Memorial Handicap	(0-70)	: Beverley	: 8 fur.	2/1
Friend James Handicap	(0-65)	: Brighton	: 8 fur.	3/1
Failford Handicap	(0-55)	: Ayr	: 7 fur.	7/2
Drayton Handicap	(0-70)	: Goodwood	: 8 fur.	5/2
Brocas Handicap	(30-75)	: Ascot	: 8 fur.	5/1
Tilburstow Handicap	(0-60)	: Lingfield	: 7 fur. 140 y.	7/4

At the beginning of the 1980 season Northleach burst through in the last furlong to snatch the valuable mile Newbury Spring Cup (35+).

Pipedreamer: Pipedreamer did not really find his best form until he was four. As a two and three-year-old nearly all his races were over five and six furlongs and it was not until he sprinted away with a 40+ 7 furlong handicap at York in the very last race of his three-year-old campaign, that the potential of the colt began to materialise. He was not on my list entering 1979 but was one of a group of what I like to call 'peripheral' horses — a few just outside the list but firmly tucked away in my memory as possibilities.

As you will see later in the book, Henry Candy trained him for the mile Royal Hunt Cup (40+) at Ascot and the colt won that race with such a devastating turn of foot, he immediately became a top priority in my plans.

The importance of Pipedreamer is not really in the amount of races he won. It is the way in which he won them that is significant. When a horse wins such a prestigious race as the 'Hunt Cup' in really brilliant quickening style, he has reached a very high level within the British handicap system. In his next race, for instance, I considered him unbeatable. Luckily in his other two wins of the season, including that next race, he was on offer, and won, at ridiculously generous prices — a fact which substantially boosted my bank. If Pipedreamers cropped up every week, we would all be millionaires in no time.

His '79 races:

Royal Hunt Cup	(40+)	: Royal Ascot	: 8 fur.	12/1
Ward Hill Bunbury Cup	(35+)	: Newmarket	: 7 fur.	15/2
William Hill Handicap	(30-35)	: Sandown	: 8 fur.	9/1

Pipedreamer did not run again in Britain.

Rhyme Royal: I have included this gelding because he is the perfect example of the type of handicapper you should be on the look-out for from the Dick Hern stable. The pattern of these animals is always the same. They are invariably big strong types that have both the build and the stamina to keep on improving throughout a season. They are mostly three and four-year-olds which have been lightly raced at two.

Rhyme Royal raced only once as a two-year-old, winning a 6 furlong maiden race at Newbury. At three he went down in his first outing but won four out of his five remaining races, improving by around 20 lbs. in doing so.

He was the type of horse that could front-run or accelerate from the rear. His 1978 wins were:

Esher Cup	(40+)	: Sandown	: 8 fur.	7/2
Sledmere Handicap	(40+)	: York	: 9 fur.	13/8
Falmouth Handicap	(35-75)	: York	: 10 fur. 110 y.	5/1
Garrowby Handicap	(45+)	: York	: 10 fur. 110 y.	8/13

Rhyme Royal won first time out in 1979 in a Sandown Park handicap. He followed this up with a Newbury handicap win. From then on he was absolutely clobbered with weight and connections unsuccessfuly aimed him at Group racing.

Royal Match: This extraordinary strong and brave late-developing handicapper is the exact type you should always be watching for.

He had only two runs as a two-year-old, on the second occasion, finishing second. At three Royal Match established himself as a consistent and genuine, but not outstanding, middle-of-the-road handicapper, notching up three victories, five seconds, and three thirds, from an exhausting fifteen runs. At four years he added a few more points to his rating with another three unspectacular handicap victories, this time from nine outings.

It was not until 1976, when he was five years old, that Royal Match really got down to business and produced the goods. One would have thought by that time, after the twenty four outings of his two previous years, the official handicappers would have had ample time to pin him down and rate him properly. But this was not the case at all.

We can only assume that through sheer guts and plenty of runs, Royal Match learned, the hard way, that winning races is about acceleration. In 1976 we saw a new animal altogether — one with a devastating burst of speed that bewildered the handicappers for the whole of the season.

Ryan Jarvis, the horse's skilful trainer, mapped out what I like to call a 'classic' campaign for the handicapper. Here are his seven victories from that 1976 season — all handicaps — all won through acceleration:

* Littlewoods Spring Cup	(45+)	: Liverpool	: 10 fur.	17/2
Sandown Cup	(50+)	: Sandown	: 10 fur.	11/4
London Gold Cup	(50+)	: Newbury	: 11 fur.	4/5
Ultramar Jubilee Stakes	(50+)	: Kempton	: 10 fur.	7/4
Bessborough Stakes	(50+)	: Royal Ascot	: 12 fur.	13/2
Great Yorkshire Handicap	(45+)	: York	: 12 fur.	11/8
Quortina Challenge Cup	(50+)	: Windsor	: 11 fur. 150 y.	Ev.

Royal Match earned a well-deserved retirement to stud in Ireland after this tremendous and highly profitable season. As I say, he was the embodiment of all I am trying to get over to you in this book.

* *n.b.* Flat racing no longer takes place at Liverpool.

Sea Chimes: This big colt is of a breed of horses even rarer than the ones with a turn of foot — front-runners that can quicken while in the lead. What's so special about this? You may ask. Well, by now you will have realised the great advantage accelerating horses have. But, in terms of the overall pace of an event, even they are always at the mercy of the horses out in front in the early stages of a race. As I said earlier, sometimes our flyers have the guts knocked out of them if they happen to run into brute force plodders. However, when you have an animal like Sea Chimes, the competent jockey can dictate the pace of a race early on before pressing the acceleration button any time he chooses in the straight. Very few rivals can cope with this kind of pace change and nine times out of ten the rest of the field (horses and jockeys) are caught on the hop and left completely bamboozled. This, in my opinion, was why Sea Chimes remained unbeaten in eight consecutive races from May 1979 until mid-season 1980, defeat finally coming after he had left handicap racing far behind and was favourite for the near £100,000 Group One Eclipse Stakes at Sandown Park.

You will see in my 'typical season' how I noted this horse the first time he won and followed his progress throughout 1979. You will also see how, because I thought I had found a similar front-running/quickening animal, I broke one of my own rules in backing the three-year-old Yellow Rock before he had won at that age. There was some downright bad luck concerning this one but he was nowhere near the valiant Sea Chimes in ability.

The Sea Chimes 1979-1980 victories:

1979

Race	Class	Course	Distance	Odds
Rutland Apprentice Handicap	(0-60)	: Newmarket	: 10 fur.	9/1
National Federation of Self Employed Handicap	(0-70)	: Newmarket	: 10 fur.	11/4
Sun Life of Canada Handicap	(0-65)	: Epsom	: 10 fur.	5/1
King George V Stakes	(45+)	: Royal Ascot	: 12 fur.	3/1

1980

Race	Class	Course	Distance	Odds
City and Suburban Handicap	(35+)	: Epsom	: 10 fur.	13/2

Race	Class	Course	Distance	Price
Sporting Chronicle Spring Handicap	(40+)	Doncaster	10 fur. 50 y.	4/5
Clive Graham Stakes (non-handicap)		Goodwood	12 fur.	13/8
Coronation Cup (Group One)		Epsom	12 fur.	5/4

These victories are up to mid-season 1980 only. (End of July).

Tesoro Mio: As I said earlier in my racecourse section, it was during a chance visit to Ayr in 1978 I spotted this tremendous little handicapper. He had already won a couple of minor non-handicap events by that time and it was clear, especially after his Ayr victory, that he was a fast improving sort with an excellent burst of finishing speed at his disposal. Although the Ayr meeting was a relatively unspectacular mid-week fixture and the races rather low in standard, my belief in the little colt was fully justified later. He won a further two handicaps in great style in 1978 and, as a four-year-old, in 1979, two more at very lucrative prices.

Here are his 1978-1979 victories:

1978

Race	Class	Course	Distance	Price
Castle Maiden Stakes (non-handicap)		Carlisle	9 fur. 80 y.	11/4
Trabroun Stakes (non-handicap)		Hamilton	8 fur. 40 y.	3/1
Cuninghame Handicap	(0-70)	Ayr	10 fur.	5/1
Darley Breweries Handicap	(35-75)	Pontefract	10 fur.	5/1
Bereford Handicap	(0-65)	Newmarket	10 fur.	5/2

1979

Race	Class	Course	Distance	Price
Ladbroke Chester Handicap	(30-75)	Chester	10 fur. 85 y.	9/1
John Smiths Magnet Cup	(40+)	York	10 fur. 110 y.	8/1

Apparently Jimmy Etherington's stable was hit by the virus earlier this year (1980) and Tesoro Mio, although well backed on a couple of occasions, so far, hasn't shown any of his old sparkle.

Town and Country: Another excellent Dick Hern late-developer. This big strong colt improved approximately 25 lbs. during his four-year-old career in 1978 and won five good handicaps in the process.

Like Royal Match, he seemed to realise what was wanted of him the more racing he had, and developed a powerful finishing thrust which kept him one step ahead of the handicapper all during the year.

As you will see. I followed him into 1979 when, unfortunately, the handicappers crucified him with weight. It was not until his eighth and second last outing that he achieved victory in a six runner non-handicap race at Ayr.

His victories in 1978 were as follows:

Newbury Summer Cup	(35+)	: Newbury	: 12 fur.	2/1
John Smith's Magnet Cup	(45+)	: York	: 10 fur. 110 y.	5/1
House of Gerard 'Coup Des Bijoux' Handicap	(45+)	: Goodwood	: 10 fur.	7/2
Chesterfield Cup	(40+)	: Goodwood	: 10 fur.	13/8
Holsten Pils Handicap	(45+)	: Doncaster	: 10 fur. 50 y.	9/4

CHAPTER 9

Breeding

In my last chapter you will notice that I have merely written the name of each horse and then proceeded with my little essay on it. In the racing papers things are slightly different. You will see, after each horse's name, other animals mentioned. This is the parentage of the horse. I left it out before so that I could explain it fully here. Taking a couple of my flyers as examples, they would appear in your paper thus:

Hang On Elvis 3 br. g. Right Tack — Prairie Princess (Sayajirao).

Northleach 4 ch. c. Northfields (USA) — Macaw (Narrator).

Let me explain this in table form:

Hang On Elvis	Name
3 br. g.	Three-year-old brown gelding.
Right Tack	Sire (father) of Hang On Elvis.
Prairie Princess	Dam (mother) of Hang On Elvis.
Sayajirao	Sire of Prairie Princess or Grand Sire (grandfather) of Hang On Elvis.

Northleach	Name.
4 ch. c.	Four-year-old chestnut colt.
Northfields	Sire (father) of Northleach.
USA	Bred in the USA.
Macaw	Dam (mother) of Northleach.
Narrator	Sire of Macaw or Grand Sire (Grandfather) of Northleach.

As you can see it is a very simple lay-out and once you are a regular reader of racing form the information will tick through your head in computer-like fashion without needing a second thought. In terms of racing parlance you will hear Jimmy Lindley or Brough Scott on TV imparting details this way:

"Northleach, a chestnut colt by Northfields out of Macaw by Narrator."

The actual breeding of racehorses is an extremely complex and precarious business. As far as our operation is concerned, very few people ever aim at breeding horses to become handicappers. Flat racing breeders invariably try for one of two types; either a sprint influenced animal for five and six furlong races, bred with the mile One and Two Thousand Guineas in mind, or, a middle distance performer that will eventually get the Derby mile and a half. Even although breeders operating on a small cut-price scale fully realise the horses they produce will probably only be capable of winning a couple of small maiden events or at most, a few handicaps, they all hold a secret hope that one day they will stumble upon a new highly successful blood-line.

Some do, and, in fact, money is not always the main prerequisite for successful breeding. Anyone involved in the bloodstock business will tell you that sheer luck, more than anything, has been the key factor in the birth of many of our champions. The history of the bloodstock business is littered with expensive failures and fairy-tale-like stories of cheap unattractive yearlings that turn out to be real crackerjacks. Nothing at all is sacred in breeding and it is not uncommon for a stallion renowned for sprinting blood to produce a long distance winner or, alternatively, a long distance stallion to produce a sprinter.

My attitude to breeding, and one I think you should adopt is;

never back an animal until it has proved itself on the racecourse no matter how much money it cost or how famous its parents were. The reverse of this must also be remembered; do not be put off a horse that has impressed you just because its blood-lines are unfashionable. Personally, if I had noted a horse bolting in at, say, the big Goodwood Meeting, I wouldn't care if its father was a Shetland Pony, in terms of backing it another time. It's the same old story; depend on your own eyes when assessing a horse's ability, only use breeding as a back-up to that.

I have always believed that the people who spend their lives within the breeding industry suffer badly from the 'cannot see the wood for the trees' syndrome when it comes to making money from backing racehorses. Far too often they risk their cash on what a horse *should* be able to do rather than what it has proved it actually *can* do. Do not fall into this trap no matter how grand a horse's parentage is or how much ballyhoo appears in the press about it.

In spite of my own attitude to breeding, certain positive facts do emerge when considering the statistics of the business. Some horses invariably make better stallions and broodmares than others and often reasonably accurate guesses can be made in relation to the distances their sons and daughters will win at. This fact is well illustrated by two popular sires of recent years; the sprinter Mummys Pet and the 1969 Derby winner Blakeney. Both these horses regularly pass on their relevant stamina influences to their progeny. Nearly all the Mummys Pet stock are endowed with the speed for five and six furlong events and as two-year-olds, they continually win early in their careers. Blakeney, on the other hand, has established himself as one of the leading producers of staying animals and, in fact, many of his stock have taken admirably to the two mile minimum National Hunt game (the jumps).

Below I have included some of the leading sires of recent years showing a *rough* guide to the progeny you would expect from them. Remember, this is only a small personal list. The scope of this book does not allow me to go into details of every sire, dam, and grand-sire, past and present. If you wish to pursue this subject further, any good class book shop can acquire for you massive volumes covering all aspects of the bloodstock business. I must add though, that usually, these works are very expensive.

The terms of reference for my list is as follows:

Sprint	:	5 fur.-6 fur. (sometimes 7 fur.)
Middle	:	8 fur.-12 fur. (sometimes 7 fur.)
Long	:	over 12 fur.

Some important sires of recent years showing the progeny you would expect from them.

Abwah	sprint	middle	—
African Sky	sprint	middle	—
Auction Ring	sprint	—	—
Balidar	sprint	—	—
Ballymore	—	middle	—
Bay Express	sprint	—	—
Be Friendly	sprint	middle	—
Blakeney	—	middle	long
Bold Lad (Ire)	sprint	middle	—
Brigadier Gerard	sprint	middle	—
Burglar	sprint	—	—
Busted	—	middle	long
Captains Gig	sprint	middle	—
Cavo Doro	—	middle	—
Comedy Star	sprint	—	—
Connaught	—	middle	—
Crepello	—	middle	—
Crowned Prince	—	middle	—
Dancers Image	sprint	—	—
Decoy Boy	sprint	—	—
Deep Diver	sprint	—	—
Derring Do	sprint	middle	—
Dike	—	middle	long
Double Jump	sprint	middle	—
English Prince	sprint	middle	—
Exbury	—	middle	long
Firestreak	—	middle	—
Forli	sprint	middle	—

Forlorn River	sprint	middle	—
Frankincense	sprint	middle	—
Gay Fandango	sprint	middle	—
Goldhill	sprint	middle	—
Good Bond	sprint	middle	—
Great Nephew	sprint	middle	—
Green God	sprint	middle	—
Gulf Pearl	—	middle	—
Habat	sprint	—	—
Habitat	sprint	middle	—
High Line	—	middle	long
High Top	sprint	middle	—
Home Guard	sprint	middle	—
Hotfoot	sprint	middle	—
Hot Spark	sprint	—	—
Huntercombe	sprint	middle	—
Irish Love	sprint	middle	—
Jimmy Reppin	sprint	middle	—
Jukebox	sprint	middle	—
Klairon	sprint	middle	—
Laser Light	sprint	middle	—
Le Levanstell	—	middle	long
Levmoss	—	middle	long
Lord Gayle	sprint	middle	—
Lorenzaccio	sprint	middle	—
Lyphard	sprint	middle	—
Majority Blue	sprint	middle	—
Manacle	sprint	—	—
Mandamus	—	middle	—
Mansingh	sprint	—	—
Martinmas	sprint	middle	—
Mill Reef	—	middle	long
Morston	—	middle	long
Most Secret	sprint	—	—
Mountain Call	sprint	—	—
Mount Hagen	sprint	middle	—
Mummys Pet	sprint	—	—

My Swallow	—	middle	long
Nijinsky	sprint	middle	—
No Mercy	sprint	middle	—
Northern Dancer	—	middle	—
Northfields	sprint	middle	—
On Your Mark	sprint	middle	—
Petingo	—	middle	—
Philip of Spain	sprint	middle	—
Pieces of Eight	sprint	middle	—
Pitcairn	sprint	middle	—
Pitskelly	sprint	middle	—
Polyfoto	sprint	middle	—
Porto Bello	sprint	—	—
Prince Regent	sprint	middle	—
Prince Tenderfoot	sprint	middle	—
Queens Hussar	sprint	middle	—
Rarity	—	middle	—
Realm	sprint	—	—
Red Alert	sprint	—	—
Red God	sprint	middle	—
Reform	sprint	middle	—
Reliance II	—	middle	long
Relko	—	middle	long
Rheingold	—	middle	—
Ribero	—	middle	long
Ridan	sprint	middle	—
Right Tack	sprint	middle	—
Roan Rocket	sprint	middle	—
Roberto	—	middle	—
Roi Soleil	sprint	middle	—
Royal And Regal	—	middle	long
Royal Palace	—	middle	—
Royal Prerogative	—	middle	—
Run The Gauntlet	—	middle	—
Sallust	sprint	middle	—
Sandford Lad	sprint	middle	—
Saulingo	sprint	—	—

Sharp Edge	sprint	middle	—
Sharpen Up	sprint	—	—
Shiny Tenth	sprint	middle	—
Silly Season	—	middle	—
Simbir	—	middle	—
Sir Ivor	—	middle	long
So Blessed	sprint	middle	—
Song	sprint	—	—
Sovereign Path	sprint	middle	—
Sparkler	sprint	middle	—
St Alphage	sprint	—	—
St Chad	sprint	middle	—
Sun Prince	sprint	middle	—
Sweet Revenge	sprint	—	—
Swing Easy	sprint	—	—
Targowice	sprint	middle	—
Thatch	sprint	middle	—
The Brianstan	sprint	—	—
The Go-Between	sprint	—	—
Tower Walk	sprint	middle	—
Town Crier	sprint	middle	—
Track Spare	sprint	middle	—
Tribal Chief	sprint	—	—
Tudor Melody	sprint	middle	—
Tudor Music	sprint	middle	—
Tumble Wind	sprint	middle	—
Tyrant	sprint	middle	—
Vaguely Noble	—	middle	—
Warpath	—	middle	long
Welsh Pageant	—	middle	—
Welsh Saint	sprint	middle	—
Wolver Hollow	sprint	middle	—

CHAPTER 10

At the Track

There is one word that sums up ninety per cent of the racecourse scene in Britain — vanity! Quite frankly the majority of people who frequent our tracks are a pain in the neck. Many of them use the racecourse as if it were their local cafe or bar — a place to pout, preen, and generally act the big-shot. I'm afraid, even in these liberal times, the racecourse reeks of class, privilege, and inequality. Everybody acts out some part or another, with the poor pretending to be well-off, the recently rich falling over themselves to let everybody know about their money, and the upper classes presiding (they think) over the whole circus — everybody tidily tucked away in their respective pens and in their proper place.

When you become a regular racegoer you will recognise each new goon as he arrives on the scene. I always do. He will swagger arrogantly past you full of pomp and importance carrying the unmistakable badges of the would-be gambler — a preposterous wide-brimmed hat and large thick cigar. As often as not there will be some fur-lined nymphomaniac in attendance.

Sometimes they last a couple of days, sometimes a couple of weeks, but the end is always the same — that distant glare in the eye of total defeat, and the little cigar stump that looks as if it has just exploded. Empty pockets, regrets, and the nymph with her eye on somebody else — why?

Because unlike us, these clowns have no long term plan of action. They arrive solely with the purpose of impressing the bird and anyone else foolish enough to be interested. They attempt, with no homework whatsoever, to back every winner of every race, every day. Their eventual sad downfall is inevitable.

From the outset, let us not make the same stupid mistakes and join the racecourse pantomime. There is plenty of time for showing off, drinking and all, in the evenings or on a Sunday. Make no mistake about it, being a professional gambler requires a working week with set hours just like any other career. As you will have already guessed, there is no one around who enjoys the pleasures of life more than me, but when it comes to Turf matters, all the nonsense has to be set aside. I must add though, that with the approach to racing I am suggesting, there is plenty of time for enjoyment and leisure. Because we are only interested in, and will be patiently waiting for, horses with certain advantageous characteristics, there is no need to be deep in form books every night seeking out bets. We can wait for the right animals to appear and when the time is right, back them.

With a sensible approach in mind then, let us plan out a racing day.

Not surprisingly, the day begins at home and I believe attire for the racecourse is vitally important. I'm not suggesting that you need a film star's wardrobe for your operation, but a little thought before you leave can pay big dividends. With horse racing being a totally outdoor sport, sometimes taking place in the most exposed places, the racegoer is always at the mercy of the unpredictable British climate. Even on the most pleasant summer's day a freak shower can make a body very uncomfortable indeed if unprepared for it. Trendy clothes can be totally unsuitable for the racetrack and often I've seen people arrive at the races radiant in their new gear only to end up like drowned rats by the end of the day. What should we wear then?

Let's start at our toes and work up.

I am going in 'feet first', as it were, because footwear is the most important item of all. A fully comprehensive day's racing requires a whole lot of walking and it you wish to get the 'feel' of the races, regular visits to the paddock to inspect the horses are essential. The paddock can sometimes be quite a way from the main stands and you will be walking back and forward there around eight times, given that a couple of races may not be of interest. Fashionable footwear can be a nightmare for this relentless plodding. Ladies! beware of those high heels!

I remember back in my early Turf days I wore a brand new pair of Italian-styled shoes to Royal Ascot where the paddock is a good walk from the betting area at the stands. I was crippled with blisters for days.

A good sensible pair of shoes (not new and well walked in) is a must, especially if it is a bit damp.

Your main suit, blazer, sport's jacket and trousers can be anything of course, although, if possible, something light-weight for mid-summer, and something a bit heavier for the Spring and late Autumn. The important thing here is some kind of light-weight raincoat that can be produced in a hurry.

One little idea I devised for the busier meetings is the zipped inside pocket, sewn so that the zip opens in an inward direction. You will eventually be carrying a lot of cash around with you and personal security is something not to be taken lightly. Remember the little mugging episode in Chichester?

Having to push a zip in towards your chest is a formidable task for any pickpocket.

Although I have already made a bit of fun out of the wide hats some idiots wear, some kind of shade from the sun is advisable. All the rails at racecourses, on the track and in the paddock, are painted in glossy white and when the sun hits them the glare can be extremely penetrating. Sunglasses are okay but can be a bit of a nuisance and, as often as not, they get lost. I personally favour the cloth cap or 'bunnet' as they call it in Scotland, but the choice is entirely your own.

Naturally it's a good idea to get yourself a pair of binoculars, but again approach the purchase with some thought. You will often find that the fat cigar people buy huge powerful binoculars far more suitable for crossing the Atlantic than going racing. You don't really need to lug anything like that around. A small pair of 8 X 30's is perfectly adequate for any racecourse and light enough not to be a burden.

When placing your bets with the bookies you will receive a numbered ticket as a receipt for your wager. This is the only proof you have that a bet has been struck at all. Obviously you cannot afford to lose it. Make sure you set a certain pocket aside for these tickets. Use the same pocket all the time so that it becomes automatic knowledge where the tickets are. Often I've seen people fumbling and stumbling with nerves looking for lost winning tickets. They cannot remember in which pocket they have placed the ticket. In their confusion it inevitably disappears altogether and all their efforts have gone for nothing. The bookies won't wear a sob-story for a minute so try and have this problem sorted out in your mind in the calm before racing. People who wear waistcoats are particularly susceptible to this pocket chaos.

No doubt you have never even considered these points I have put forward in relation to attire. The thing is, if you are going to become a gambler, do it thoroughly and systematically. You must be able to stalk the racecourse completely relaxed and in comfort. Nothing about your clothing should be irritating you.

Let me ask you a question: When you leave for the shipyard, coal mine, or office, in the morning, do you ever consider taking your wife and children with you? Of course you don't. Well, apply the same rule when you are going racing. Go it alone. If other people are with you their wants and needs quite rightly have to be taken care of and far too much of your valuable and expensive time will be taken up waiting in endless queues for gins and tonic, hamburgers, and lemonade. You cannot hope to be efficient at the game if you are acting host as well as trying to get everything out of the racing. Arrange to meet your family and friends later in the evening just as you would do in any other job. Do not look upon it as being unkind. Your family, more than anyone, will benefit if your operation at the racecourse is well organised and successful.

One racing acquaintance of mine feels even more vehemently about his companions than I do. He told me once about his ideal gambler's wife — 'a 36-24-36 blonde deaf and dumb landlady of a pub in Newmarket'.

Let us move on then. We are comfortably turned out and on our way — alone. If you are travelling by car, aim at arriving at the track about an hour before racing. This will allow ample time to dump your coat or bag in the cloakroom, have a tidy up or even a *soft* drink, and be at the paddock to see the horses parading before the first race.

If you are using public transport, then obviously the same time schedule applies, although here we have to be a bit more careful. Do not get involved in any card games on the train (coming home in particular). Many a naïve beginner has been cleaned out this way long before he ever gets a chance to bet on the horses. Neither should you pay any attention whatsoever to any kind of tips or supposed inside information. Even if you end up sitting beside bookmakers, close your ears and stick rigidly to your own plans. I am acquainted with some of the course bookies and, while they may be masters at manipulating and shifting odds around, many of them are the world's worst tipsters. There own operation is aimed at making a profit no matter what horses win. Consequently, their opinion of individual animals matters little. If you have watched a race carefully and been impressed by a horse, do not let anything change your mind about what you have seen. Making money from gambling is all about having the guts to back up your own opinion.

And your's will be a well thought out opinion — stick to it!

There are usually three tiers of accommodation at a racecourse; The Club or Members' Enclosure, Tattersalls Enclosure, and the Silver Ring. For our purposes the Silver Ring is out. This is the cheapest part of the course and nearly always situated well down the track from the winning post. There is no access to the paddock, and all that can be seen of the horses is a streaky blur as they flash past. Quite frankly, you would be just as well catered for in a high street bookmaker's shop

The top tier at the track is the Club or Members' Enclosure. Entrance here will cost around £5.50-£6.00 for a daily members' badge or you can apply for annual membership at around £40-£50. The yearly arrangement can be quite a bargain if you are a regular visitor to a particular track. For annual members a metal badge is issued which does for the year. With both daily and yearly badges, every part of the racecourse is accessible to you except the private boxes which are rented on a yearly basis at places like Epsom and Ascot. I don't think you need concern yourself with a private box at the moment. They are ultra expensive and often applied for by business firms rather than individuals.

Tattersalls Enclosure is where all the action takes place. Entrance is around the £4 mark nowadays. The bookmakers are situated in 'Tats' and all the betting and price manoeuvring goes on there.

There is a set of bookmakers apart from the main body of the 'ring' known as 'rails bookies', so called because they are set up in a line all down the rail between the Members' Enclosure and Tattersalls. You will find, 'on the rails', all the main representatives of the big old established firms like Hills, Ladbrokes, Heathorns, etc. They act in much the same way as our big clearing banks and most of the really important bets end up with them. These firms can stand huge losses if necessary but like you and I, they work on a 'long run' basis and make a handsome profit over the period of each year — they wouldn't be there otherwise.

As you will see from the diagram of a typical racecourse included on page (123), there are two other facilities for betting at the track. There is a Tote building, run by the Horse Totalisator Board, and a betting shop run on the same basis as a high street outfit.

The Tote operates a pool system based on the amount of money taken for each race. The major drawback here is that you do not know what you will receive in winnings until the dividend is declared over the loudspeakers after each race. This dividend can go either way in relation to the eventual starting price of a winning or placed horse; it can pay more, or less, than the equivalent bet struck with the bookies or in the betting shop.

It is very much a case of swings and roundabouts although the rule of thumb seems to be, steer clear of the Tote if backing a popular jockey like Piggott, Carson, or Mercer. The dividend tends to be a bit lower on the horses ridden by these experts simply because more people select them to win and the pool has to be shared further. I suggest that you forget the Tote and course betting shop and stick to trying to get good prices from individual bookies, remembering, of course, what I have already written about not being able to pay tax beforehand at the track. (Deductions — bookies, 4% — track betting shop, 6% — Tote, taken account of in dividend).

Now let us move on to paddock inspection. This is a must for the shrewd racegoer. Even if we are not betting in a race we must still view the horses before the races run over our distances. If, for instance, you observe beforehand that only seventy-five per cent of a certain field are fit, then obviously the merit of the winner must be assessed with this in mind. On the other hand, if you are impressed by a winner that has burst clear of a fully-fit field, then the chances

PADDOCK INSPECTION

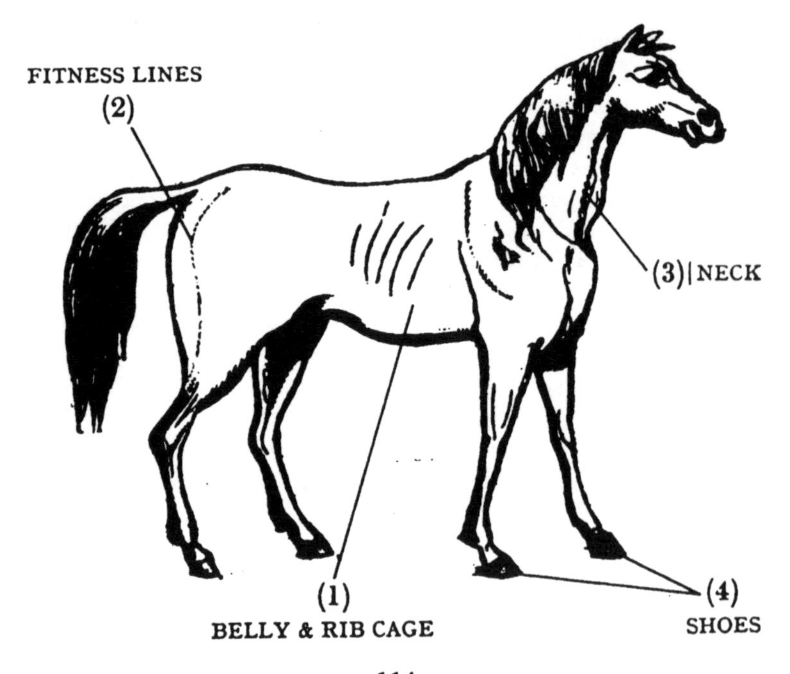

are you have found a sure future winner. This overall fitness of fields is particularly relevant at the beginning of a season in March and April. Then, an easy winner can be considerably over-rated, although if the same winner reappears within a few days, then he is quite likely to again meet only half-fit rivals. You must learn to weigh these points up for yourself. Never forget that unfit horses do not win races. They won't be expected to. Apply this knowledge to the chances of the high street punter — he hasn't a hope in hell of ever knowing what he is doing. This is exactly why I keep on raving about seeing things with your own eyes and acting upon them.

How can we tell if a horse is fit? There are certain automatic points to look out for.

1. Observe closely the horse's belly. The fit horse will be well tightened up there — no loose flab or obvious fat. Look out for the prominence of the rib-cage. (See diag.)
2. Look at the horse's rear end for the fitness lines down its behind. This area should again be tight and well muscled. (See diag.)
3. The neck and coat of the horse should be gleaming and hard. (See diag.)
4. Have a look at the type of shoes a horse is wearing. The thick steel plates a horse wears for exercise at home are heavy and cumbersome. If the animal still has them on at the track, the chances are, the stable are not trying with him. Look for the light aluminium plates that most triers wear. Occasionally you will see a horse with aluminium at the front and steel at the back. Trainers sometimes use this set-up to combat particular ground conditions. Naturally, when you see this, closer attention to the other points of the horse are necessary to determine fitness. (See diag.)
5. Many people judge horses by the way they walk. A 'good walker's' hind footprint will overlap the print made by his forelegs. In my opinion, this kind of observation is more relevant to judging, say, two-year-old newcomers, rather than animals with already proven ability. If I noted a horse that had impressed me greatly in victory, I wouldn't care if it

walked round the paddock like John Cleese entering the Ministry of Funny Walks.

6. Watch out for a horse sweating badly. Horses that break out in sweat invariably use up a lot of important energy in doing so. As often as not, they do not show their best form on the racecourse afterwards. Do not be too concerned about a little dampness around the neck. This is only a sign of the horses winding up a bit and raring to go. It is below the saddle sweat that is much more serious, in and around the horse's rear quarters and belly.
7. Do not be put off a horse because it looks a bit small in comparison to its rivals. My theory is one many a successful football manager has adopted: if they're good enough, they're big enough. The record books are full of brilliant small horses.
8. When the horses file out of the paddock, follow them down to the track and watch them cantering down to the post. Often the plus marks we have made in a horse's favour in the paddock can be cancelled out if the animal does not stride out well to the post. The horse trained to win will glide down effortlessly with a nice fluent action whereas with unfit horses, it is not difficult to spot that they have been under-galloped. Be careful not to confuse 'going down badly' with the jockey stopping the horse from bolting. In some cases, with younger animals and late developers, the horse thinks it should be charging away as soon as it is out of the paddock. The good jockey will have a vice-like grip on his reins to prevent this. I am afraid you will have to put in a few hours practice before you can benefit from watching the horses heading down to the start.

   All this 'going to post' takes place very quickly by the way, and it becomes quite hopeless sorting them out if five or six horses charge past together. Try and concentrate on your own animal if this happens. It's good re-affirmation for your plans if the selection glides down in style.

I must add right now that none of these paddock points can be taken as fool-proof. In my time I have seen winners covered in sweat in the pre-race paddock, winners wearing only their training shoes, fat winners, and winners that have gone to post dismally. A horse's chance of winning any given race quite naturally depends on the fitness of its rivals. If they are a particularly bad lot or are all unfit then anything can happen. Just try to use the paddock as a back up. Do not, I repeat *not,* use paddock observations for actually finding winners. You may get away with it once or twice but in the *long run* you will be wiped out. Some horses have all the looks, breeding, and paddock credentials, but just cannot run fast or accelerate. Eventually you will start backing them. If you are going to bet on horses before you have seen what they can do, why not train as a Kamakaze pilot, you'll get a far bigger kick out of destroying yourself that way.

Bob Sievier, one of the greatest gamblers in the history of the Turf, wrote in his autobiography around the turn of the century: 'Owners, trainers, and every man who helps to support racing, are bled dry by aliens to the sport'. He was outraged at having to pay £2 for a room at Doncaster.

Well I'm afraid little has changed in the past eighty years.

Whatever you do at the racecourse, don't get into the habit of buying a lot of snacks, dinners, or drinks, there. The prices are ridiculous and the fiddling that goes on behind counters is, in my opinion, nothing short of a national scandal.

When you become a regular you will notice that many of the bookies and their employees bring along their own flasks of tea and sandwiches. I personally never need more than an orange drink at the track but if you feel that a little snack picks you up a bit in mid-afternoon, then take along your own pre-prepared food. It is not so important for the casual racegoer of course, but being a regular can be very costly if you continually wine and dine at the mercy of racecourse caterers.

Onward then. We will assume that we know our way around the racecourse. What about the actual placing of a bet there? As I mentioned earlier, for this we go into 'Tats' and wage war on the bookies. I do not use 'war' unintentionally by the way. Forget all about the beautiful scenery, warm sunshine, and shimmering trees. Adopt the 'kill or be killed' philosophy immediately. There is only one reason why all those bookies are there — to get your money. Never forget that.

With almost any other job you can make the occasional blunder and get away with it — British politics and industry show this only too well. However, our game is a bit different. The professional gambler's lot is like that of the goalkeeper. One mistake, and disaster is tapping you on the shoulder like a ghoul.

It is hard to explain on paper the atmosphere when the betting market is 'live'. People leap around all over the place trying to get the odds they're after, sometimes actually knocking each other down in the process. Many of the old heads use this mêlée to create false market moves.

Somebody suddenly appears in a panic desperate to get cash on a certain animal. The bookie takes the bet and hurriedly rubs the price off his board. Down comes the 5/1 and up goes 4/1. Now the rush really starts. 3/1, 5/2, 2/1 — people are actually fighting with each other to bet their cash. Meanwhile the bookies' real fancy is quietly drifting out in price so that people will be put off backing it. I've seen these tactics so often, it's not true. This is a favourite bookies' move when they are faced with a genuinely fancied runner from a non-gambling stable. They knock the price out so that everyone thinks there is something wrong with the animal. A false favourite is created to take its place and soak up all the 'mug' money — and there is plenty of that around.

I said just now the 'bookies' real fancy'. Take note of that. For goodness sake don't become a party to the ridiculous theory that the bookies 'know' what will win horse races. If anybody knew this for certain there would be no betting industry at all. The whole show revolves round the uncertainty of the sport. The bookies, like us, form an opinion, weigh up the possibilities, and lay out their books accordingly. Certainly they know where the money is going, but in no way do they have any mystic qualities which gives them an advantage over anybody. A good sensible bank protects *them* too from disastrous days.

One thing you must never do when you reach 'Tats' is change your selection for something else that appears to be attracting loads of money. Nothing that happens out there among the bookies will have changed the ability of your horse. It won't have lost its courage or accelerating powers just because there is a mountain of cash going on to one of its rivals. All these betting manoeuvres are geared for Mr Average Racecourse Punter. Let me tell you about him.

The first thing he does when he arrives at the track is head for a pint. Thereafter he drifts between the bar and the bookies all afternoon, never visiting the paddock once. He has not even considered the day's horses until he is at the track. He tries to be a shrewd customer and blindly follows all the betting moves I have just described. He has no chance of winning over a long period, being at the mercy of all the trickery under the sun and duly paying the price. I myself did the same stupid things years ago but soon realised I was being kidded along like an idiot. I'm saving you a fortune in these few lines by informing you that it is impossible to win at racing by betting this way. It is not the prices that win races it's the horses.

You will hear often gamblers talking about 'value' in betting. Getting good value simply means getting a better price for a horse than you expected. If you arrive down beside the bookies and are decidedly unhappy about the price offered for your fancy, then simply give it a miss and keep your money for another day. This is not easy at first and takes a bit of self-discipline. It is particularly galling when your selection actually wins. But consider it in the same light as purchasing a new coat. If you think the price is outrageous then you don't buy. It's the same with betting.

I always remember trying to convince a chap at a party that betting odds-on shots was a mug's game. His theory was that backing dead certs was the only way to win at racing. That is backing, say, five to one on shots (1/5) — putting on £500 to win £100 (£600 return). I'm damned if I could convince him that if only one out of five bets at that price was beaten, all his profit would be cancelled out.

This, of course, is an extreme example on value but a simpler way to consider it is this: If you back a 6/1 winner, the profit margin, in terms of the growth of the bank and even after a couple of losing bets, is still very healthy indeed.

I myself favour something in the 4/1-10/1 region although occasionally I will go a bit lower if I think I have found an outstanding horse. Naturally, when seeking out prices, you will sometimes blunder; like taking 3/1 about a horse that ends up 5/1. In these circumstances keep calm and try to shut the longer odds out of your mind. It is time to start believing in yourself again. If you struck such a bet at 3/1 you were obviously, at the time, quite happy about the price. Stick to the theory that you received good odds. Stock marketeers and many other businessmen face this kind of problem daily and have to have great courage to survive. Once you have made your decision get up into the stands, find a good viewing position, and forget about the bookmakers.

When one of your horses bolts in you then have to set about collecting your winnings. Again plan out every move. Your ticket should be at the ready. I always note, on the back side of it, the price received and the money involved (winnings less tax).

Your bookmaker will not automatically pay out your cash, he will ask you how much you want. If your calculations are wrong and you ask for less than the correct amount, then you receive what you ask for. If you ask for more you'll be told to f★ck off. Get this little sum right for goodness sake and watch every move while the money is counted into your palm.

Once you have your cash, keep it in a tightly clenched fist and head for the best toilet at the track. Lock yourself in a cubicle and get sorted out — money tucked safely out of harm's way and jacket zipped or buttoned. If you are new to the game, sit for a moment and calm down. Then back out to look for future winners. Do *not* use your winnings to dabble in races you have not prepared for. If you find the temptation overwhelming, go home and get drunk. It's a lot cheaper than continuing betting.

If your selection has blown out, your stake is down the drain, and you are miles away from home, then don't despair. There is still a chance to turn a minus into a plus. All is not lost for your evening's entertainment.

If, in a later race, an outsider is sprinting away inside the final furlong, get into a good central position on the green just at the winning post. The stands will be deathly silent. Start cheering the outsider home; 'Go on my son! Go on my son!' All the heads will jerk round to see who this shrewd bugger is. Among the heads there is always some mercenary little dolly, heart set on an evening out with all the trimmings. It's a real eye-opener how easy it is to chat them up in the bar after racing.

Remember, do not lose interest in the racing just because you have no money involved. It may well be in the very last race of the afternoon that the future star appears. Even if it doesn't and you mark off all the runners in that race as fully fit but exceedingly mediocre, the information will invariably be of great importance for some future event. If considering one of our horses for a race, it is very re-assuring if you have already taken note of, and written off, most of its rivals as one-paced. The chance of a shock result becomes more remote if you already know all the animals in a field through observation.

No doubt after a big mid-afternoon win you will be bursting with enthusiasm for the game. Your pen will be red hot making paddock and race-reading notes. It is a slightly different story after a mid-afternoon defeat. You will be cursing everything upside down, including me, and your main thought will be to get to hell out of the track.

When this occurs try and take comfort in the 'long run' theory. The plan is still well thought out and logical — nothing has changed that. Every job has its unpleasant side and when you are just starting out on the Turf, the empty sick feeling of defeat is worse than anything I know.

Train yourself to shrug off defeat and move on. Make notes for the future. You will be surprised how often a race you walked out on becomes a vital factor in a forthcoming event. It is really maddening when you realise that after all the expense and preparation, you missed it because of illogical and negative thinking.

Now let us move on to race-reading. A good question to ask yourself in this respect is 'can horses that have won, win again?' This is vitally important for us. It can be taken further: in what fashion did they win ? can they accelerate or were they merely whipped to victory? At the winners' enclosure, did the horse win with ease or was it blowing the house down?

All these points can be noted without the involvement of betting. In fact, they can be done more efficiently when no money is involved. When a load of your cash is running on a horse it is quite natural to watch it fanatically to the exclusion of every other runner — even to the exclusion of a better horse. When there is no bet, a race can be viewed as a whole with no bias towards individual animals.

Many racing scribes rave on about, and base their selections on, horses that 'show promise' in their races. You have probably read their articles and know all the stock clichés:

'He was running on well at the finish'

'She was a good second'

'He is gradually improving'

'She'll be better for the race'

'A longer distance will suit him better'

'A win is just round the corner'

'He's knocking at the door'

The common denominator throughout these phrases is that all the horses involved are losers. Never pay any attention to this drivel unless a horse is already on your list. Concern yourself only with winners and the way in which they won. Our whole operation is based on impressive winners, not on studying form books and crystal ball gazing.

That, my friends, is the world of the racecourse. No matter what can be said for it or against it, one thing is certain — it is a world that is alive and, if you are involved totally in the sport, as I am, you will be alive also. It is an ever changing world with no time for moaning losers or hypocrite do-gooders. It's every man for himself. Stay alive or die — quite simple — no complications.

On page (123) I have included a plan of a 'standard' racecourse. It is a rough layout based on features common to most tracks. Some courses have, in recent years, eliminated the Silver Ring and combined it with Tattersalls Enclosure. Lingfield Park is a good example of this.

Key to Diagram

1. Public Car Park — On some occasions free, some pay.

AT THE TRACK

PLAN OF STANDARD RACECOURSE

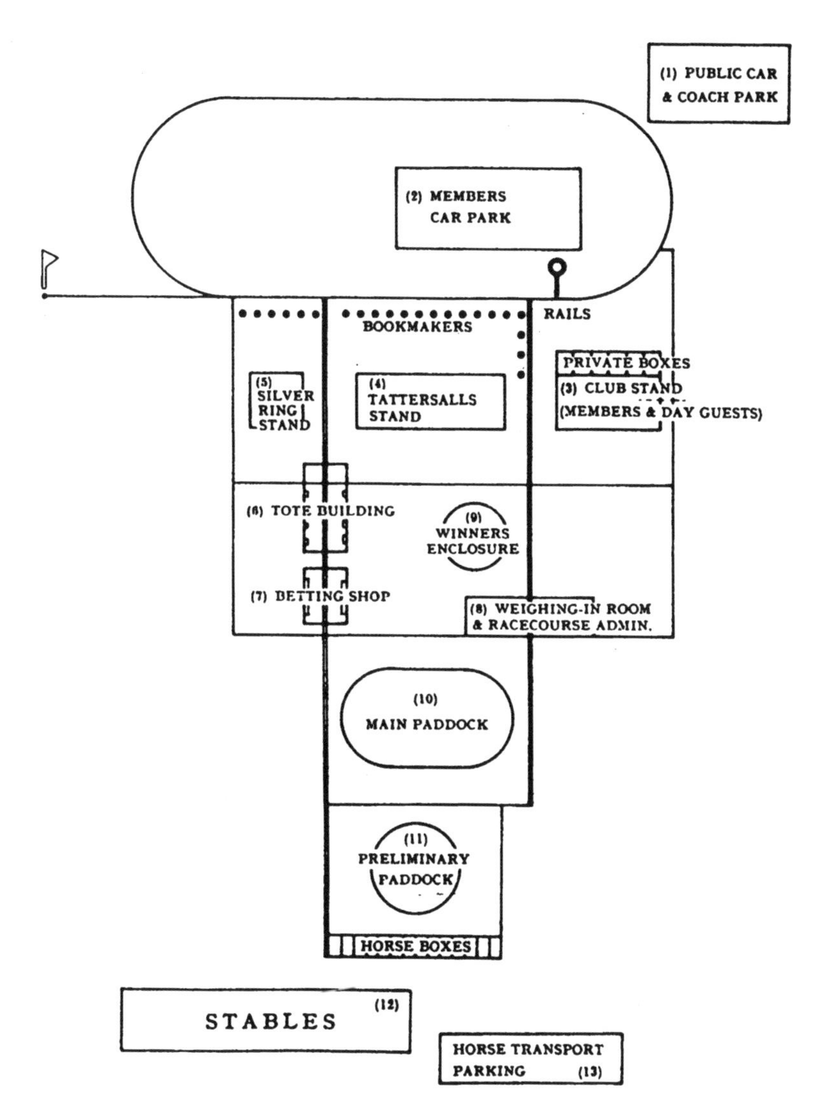

2. Members' Car Park	Usually combined with yearly membership.
3. Club (Members') Stand & Enclosure	Entrance by a yearly badge (approx. £40-£50 or by daily membership approx. £6). Bars, buffet, restaurant, champagne bars, private boxes. Access to all parts of the course. During Royal Ascot week and on Derby day at Epsom, yearly members and selected guests only. Formal dress compulsory.
4. Tattersalls Stand & Enclosure	Entrance approx. £4. Big bookmaking firms (rails) and individual bookies situated here. Bars, buffet, sometimes restaurant. Access to Tote building, betting shop, winners' enclosure, paddocks. *No access to Members' Enclosure*
5. Silver Ring Stand	Entrance approx. £2. Smaller bookmakers. Access to Tote building, betting shop, bars, buffet, sometimes fish and chips bar. *No access to Tattersalls or Members'*
6. Tote Building	Worked on a pool system with allocated tickets and declared tax paid dividends. 50p, £1, & £5 windows offering singles, place only bets, forecasts (1st & 2nd), combinations, daily double, daily treble, and Tote Jackpot at main meeting of day. Tote Jackpot (all six winners).
7. Betting Shop	Same basis as high street bookmakers although tax is deducted at 6% (6p in the £) from winnings. *Tax cannot be paid when placing a bet.*

8. Weighing-in Room & Racecourse	Jockeys' changing rooms etc.
Administration	All paper work of racecourse.
9. Winners' Enclosure	First, second, and third, paraded here after each race. Presentation of trophies, press, owners, trainers.
10. Parade Ring or Main Paddock	Horses paraded here before each race. Owners, trainers, jockeys, & officials only in middle of parade ring.
11. Preliminary Parade Ring or secondary paddock	Horses exercised, washed down, saddled, before main parade ring and race.
12. Stables	Horses taken here when arriving at course.
13. Horse Transport Parking	Vans, horse boxes, etc.

CHAPTER 11

Final Thoughts

Well friends, this is how it's done. There are no doubt other winning formulas, but this is mine. No systems, guessing games, or precarious classic races; just plain common sense based on observation, past performances, and a thorough understanding of the handicap system. You can see from the next chapter, that I have my share of bad luck and downright wrong decision-making, but under the protection of the 'bank' it is all comfortably taken care of. As I said right at the beginning of the book; anyone can back winners, but making a profit from them is an entirely different matter. In gambling, the lay-out of the cash you have available is by far the most important part of the operation. Make no mistake about it, the bookies you are trying to outwit use exactly the same tactics. They are most certainly not invincible and, although many don't realise it, on any given race day, some bookie or another will take a right old hammering. Did you know, for instance, that at the track, *they* are all betting against one another too? Well, they are, so don't for goodness sake adopt the idea that bookmakers are all in league with each other against the poor little punter. That is all just 'sore loser' talk. Out there among these men it is quite literally a case of 'dog eat dog'. There is never any quarter given when gambling for high stakes.

You will see from the chart of the bank that I really coined it in and set the seal on things around the July and early August period. As any successful horse racing gambler will tell you, this is a familiar pattern, especially after a good long spell of dry weather. The form settles down and the good horses that have been trained to reach their peak then, really turn it on. After a couple of seasons you will see this trend emerging yourself. Try and make sure that you too are fit and alert in mid-summer, so that some of those rare 'golden' weeks don't slip past you. *Never go on holiday during this period.* A gambling season is a complete entity. You start off cautiously, get the 'feel' of the form, ground, etc., hit a peak, and then gradually tail off. To disrupt this delicate chain by going off to lie in Spain for a couple of weeks is suicidal. By the time you get home and back into the groove again, the season will be nearly gone and you will find yourself desperately trying to piece something together during the notorious 'back end' when the heavy rain will be rearing its ugly head again and playing havoc with the form. And anyway, all those warm continental holiday resorts are far more pleasant, and cheaper, in the off-peak seasons.

I would like to say a few words about using the video in conjunction with your gambling campaign.

If you are going to use TV form to plan out your bets, make sure you do not write off two or three horses just because you do not have them down on tape. It is very easy to favour animals you *do* have on film, often to the exclusion of better ones.

TV racing in this country is unequalled in quantity or quality, but all TV companies are governed both by money and the amount of racing they are allowed to cover. Following the pattern of the Press and general public interest, they quite naturally incline towards the Classic-type races for their programmes. However, even here their coverage can be incomplete and rather limiting. Let me give you a couple of examples of what I mean.

In 1979 the BBC and ITV between them covered practically every lead-up race to the Derby except the one which threw up the eventual winner of the race. Troy's mid-week victory in the Predominate Stakes at Goodwood was not covered by any of the companies.

It was the same story in the run-in to the 1980 One Thousand Guineas. The key race a couple of weeks before the big one was the Fred Darling Stakes at a Newbury Friday meeting where Millingdale Lillie beat Mrs Penny into second place with Quick As Lightning third. Newbury is a BBC venue and; in fact, they covered racing there the following afternoon (Sat). The result of the One Thousand Guineas was as follows: Quick As Lightning first; Our Home second; Mrs. Penny third; and Millingdale Lillie fourth.

I am not for a minute suggesting incompetence on the part of the TV companies, in fact, the two examples above were downright bad luck, but be careful with TV form, it can sometimes be very misleading.

I think that's just about it. As you can see, I combine my racing and gambling with having a bloody good time and, more importantly, a bloody good laugh. Don't ever lose your sense of humour or become the archetypal gambler you see at the movies — a moody slant-eyed method actor with tiresome Clint Eastwood cigar stuck between the lips. Certainly keep you wits about you and take as much cash out of the game as you can, but for god's sake remain human. After all, what's the sense of making a fortune if you can't enjoy yourself spending it?

Good luck to you all

Stewart Simpson

APPENDIX

A Typical Season

Normally at this point in any racing publication the writer fills up space in the remaining pages with a whole load of junk in the form of glossaries, systems, the Queen's Horses, the History of the Turf, and anything else that comes into his head to produce a few more words.

Not here friends!

I am going to show you how it's done. A complete season's gambling based on my own efforts a couple of years ago (1979). It was not a spectacular year by any means but as you will see, a reasonably profitable one — an average year I would say. Without any messing around then lets get on with it. £1,000 bank (20 units @ £50) + £1,000 expenses.

Sat. March 24: The first important race of the year for handicap men is the Lincoln (45+) at Doncaster. It is always a big field and the draw plays an important part over the straight mile race. The ground last year was soft and I gave the race a miss betting-wise. The eventual winner Fair Season was one of a short list of horses I had picked out as possibilities. It had a particularly good season in 1978 winning four handicaps, but had notched up some poor efforts too. He had never been added to my special list.

On the day though, he produced a good burst of speed to win by an impressive 3 lengths. As I said earlier somewhere; early season runaway winners must be treated with caution and the Lincoln is no exception. In a way it was a predictable result, and predictable results, in my opinion, are victories for the handicapper — no new promising blood if you know what I mean. The vital draw at Doncaster throws even more suspicion on a result there. Ninety per cent of the time high numbers are best and the 1979 result bore the fact out well. The first three were drawn 15, 22, and 23 respectively, from a field of 23 runners.

I watched the Doncaster meeting on television.

Sat. April 7: Salisbury was my first meeting of the year and what a bloody day it turned out to be! Weather wise it was one of the worst days I've ever experienced at a racecourse. The heavens opened and many could have done with my little tit-bits on dress. Hundreds gave up watching the racing altogether soon after the meeting started and the bars and restaurant areas were packed out with cold shivering bodies. The trouble was, that for many, there was just nowhere to go. A massive crowd turned out to see the debut of newcomer Steve Cauthen. Goodness knows what the young American thought of our weather. He must have wished he had stayed at home. Salisbury, shortly before, having attained Group Two status, was completely unprepared for the thousands who arrived. The ground all round the paddock area turned to thick mud and I'll wager more than a few pairs of shoes never saw daylight again.

Once again I did not bet. I was not impressed by any of the horses either — not even Marquee Universal, Cauthen's winning mount in the first race (40+ h'cap). I had a good laugh to myself that afternoon though. It was over the Two Thousand Guineas Trial Stakes, a Group Three race intended as a guide to the eventual Two Thousand Guineas at Newmarket in April. Not my territory at all, but I went to the paddock for observations anyway. Some of these classic prospects turn out to be good handicappers when they lower their sights a bit. It's a good idea to keep an eye on them.

The eventual winner of the race caught my eye right away in the preliminary paddock — Lake City, trained by Ryan Price and ridden by Brian Taylor. The big colt glided down to the post effortlessly rain, mud, and all. It came back exactly the same way and won easily by 3 lengths at 12/1, the race taking place in an eery silence because of the tannoy system clapping out.

I then saw this chap throwing away his race card in disgust and storming into the bar. I picked up the card out of the mud. It was one of the Timeform Organisation's cards costing around £2, with supposed information regarding the characteristics of each animal. Part of the commentary on Lake City read as follows:

"Has a very smooth, daisy-cutting action which probably isn't suited to a soft surface".

See what I mean about checking horses out first before deciding just what they can do? There were certainly no daisies around that afternoon.

I got back to London as soon as I could at night. What a wash-out!

Sat. April 14: The Easter Meeting at Kempton Park, and especially the Rosebury Handicap (45+), is a must for our operation. Good horses always turn out for this long-standing 10 furlong race. Peter Walwyn's Proven, a four-year-old, eventually won it after a long struggle with Better Blessed, a well tested five-year-old. There was only ¾ length in it and I was a bit disappointed that the result had not been more decisive. Pat Eddery had to work like the devil on Proven and I could not really note the horse for a future win unless he was substantially dropped in class.

Mon. April 16: Second day of the Kempton meeting and a couple of horses caught my eye. In the first race, a 10 furlong handicap for three-year-olds (0-70), the John Dunlop/Willie Carson duo swung into action. Lohengrin, a lightly-raced two-year-old, came with a lovely little burst to take the race with ease at 8/1. I noted him as sure to improve further.

Later in the afternoon in a mile handicap for the older horses (30-75), I was really impressed by Black Minstrel, a five-year-old also ridden by Willie Carson. The horse was held up (a sign I like to see) and came with a terrific burst just around the furlong pole. He won by 2½ lengths and looked as if he could have made it six.

Black Minstrel only carried 7st. 11 lbs. in the race which meant he had a pretty low official rating. When I checked him out in the form book at home that evening, I found he had done little before. But the thing many punters fail to recognise is that some horses do not really mature until they are four or five. That evening Black Minstrel went straight into the notebook as a sure future betting opportunity. Five-year-old or not, I had seen him flying in with my own two eyes.

Tues. Wed. Thurs. April 17, 18, 19: Off to Newmarket for the Craven Meeting. Everyone was there to see the great Tromos romp away with the Craven Stakes (Group 3), another run-up race to the Two Thousand Guineas. He flopped at 30/100 (approx 3/1 on) and more than one racegoer left there and then sick as parrots. Tromos had been backed ante-post all through the winter for the 'Guineas'.

The whole carry on meant little to me. I was more interested in the three-year-old handicap (30-75) which followed the big race. I was very impressed by the 4 length winner Chalet, a Cecil/Mercer animal. The horse strode away in great style to win from a big field on the straight 7 furlong course.

There were no further horses for the notebook during the three days although the finish of the Tote Free Handicap for three-year-olds was very controversial. Lester Piggott made a right mug of his ride on Jeroboam, getting boxed in on the inside of the field. When an opening eventually did appear for him it was far too late. Pat Eddery already had the race sewn up on the favourite, Lyric Dance. This was another 7 furlong event by the way.

Even Lester can make mistakes — at Newmarket too. If there's one thing in abundance there, it's plenty of room. It just re-affirms what I said earlier about working on a *long-run* basis. Anything can happen in an individual race.

One horse that did impress me very much at the meeting was One In A Million. She won the 'Nell Gwyn' (a similar race to the Craven only for fillies going for the Thousand Guineas) in great style with a fantastic turn of foot. I was sure that day she would eventually win the big race in May. Not my field of operation though. For all I knew there may have been an equally brilliant filly in Ireland or France.

You have obviously noticed that I still hadn't backed anything by the end of the Craven Meeting. Why should I? There is plenty of time in a season stretching from March to November. Patience is an invaluable weapon for the professional gambler.

Talking about weapons by the way, I stayed over in Cambridge for two nights that week and ended up at a real weird students' party on the Wednesday. It had gone normally enough (records, snacks, drinks) until about eleven o'clock when two of the lady guests emerged from a bedroom in black leather gear. You should have seen the bloody great whips they had. It was all only supposed to be a joke right enough.

I laughed heartily with everyone else, got my coat, the bottle of champagne I had brought, and bailed out sharpish. I've experienced little jokes like that before. The humour disappears rapidly when they start asking for volunteers to be tied up and gagged.

Fri. Sat. April 20, 21: There was nothing at all for the notebook on Friday or Saturday at Newbury although I was quite impressed by Brians Venture's win in the Playboy Bookmakers' Newbury Spring Cup (45+). It was a gutsy performance rather than brilliant, the horse battling on gamely to win by 2 lengths.

Mon. April 23: I gave the Brighton Meeting a miss. I sometimes like going for the top-weights there but not on softish ground which it was that day.

Tues. Wed. Thurs. April 24, 25, 26: As I have mentioned, the Epsom Spring Meeting is one of my favourite meetings of the year. The Derby Meeting can be exceedingly hot and sticky, but strolling over the Downs in April is like having a good spring cleaning. All the winter cobwebs are blown away and the mind begins to sharpen for the months ahead. Very refreshing indeed.

On the first day two top-weight handicappers won. They were actually joint top weights with other horses. It was in keeping with my theories about Epsom but both were three-year-old races, one over 7 furlongs and the other 10 furlongs. I had not noted any of the two animals before so naturally I did not plunge in. Neither of them were particularly impressive in victory.

Another point to remember when considering Epsom is the reverse side to my theory of it being an easy track. With the course being advantageous to the top-weighted animals, the form there is often not corroborated on other, particularly difficult, tracks. Put it this way; if a horse cannot win there carrying a certain weight (given that it is not the track itself which stops it), then it is unlikely to succeed at Ascot or Newbury.

Nothing of note on the Wednesday although Doogali, the 25/1 winner of the City and Suburban Handicap (40+), was one of my short list for the Lincoln. The horse was twentieth of twenty three at Doncaster and always seemed to need firm to show his best. There is no way it could have been backed at Epsom although Williams, Doogali's Scottish trainer, must have fancied it, coming all the way down from Ayr for the race.

Thursday was the day of my first wager. Black Minstrel turned out for the Crown Plus Two Apprentice Championship Handicap (phew!) for four-year-olds and upwards (0-80) over the 7 furlongs 11 yards course. He was carrying a 5 lbs penalty for his Kempton win which I considered completely inadequate to stop him going in again. He had already won over 7 furlongs in 1978 and Epsom again provided the softish ground he seemed to need.

That's what I call a bet; good quickening powers, ground conditions right, and moderate rivals. The 0-80 field was very similar indeed to the 0-70 lot at Kempton. In fact, some of the same horses were taking part again.

With Epsom being very tricky, the only thing I was worrying about was the big field, especially with all the horses apprentice ridden. You very seldom get everything one hundred per cent in you favour though and, after weighing up all the pro's and con's, I decided to have a plunge. The pilot, young Walter Swinburn, was as good, if not better, than any of the other jockeys in the field. I managed to get 5/1 although after my bet and some others, the price dropped and ended at 3's.

Black Minstrel did exactly the same as he did at Kempton, coming with a great run in the final yards to snatch the race. A good start to the season.

Stake	*Return (after 4% tax)*	*Actual Winnings*	*Bank (£1,000)*
£50	£288	£238	£1,238

Fri. Sat. April 27, 28: The first day of the weekend meeting at Sandown offered another great betting opportunity, Rhyme Royal, a four-year-old trained by Dick Hern and ridden by Willie Carson, turned out for the Sandown Cup (40+) over 10 furlongs for the older animals. The horse was one of my list from 1978 and although this was only its first outing of the year, I decided to plunge in. Why?

As I said earlier in my summing up of Sandown Park, I believe the top-weights have a big advantage there. Rhyme Royal was top-weighted with 10 stone — a full 15 lbs. heavier than the next horse in the handicap. When you see a big gap like this between top-weights and their rivals it indicates a horse far superior in ability to the rest of the field. It is only a question of whether the allotted weight can stop it or not (slow it down). On a turning track like Sandown you must always consider such an animal, particularly if it is from a good stable and has previously proved its ability to your satisfaction. In this case Rhyme Royal had everything going for it.

1. Willie Carson.
2. Trainer Dick Hern is well known for first time out winners.
3. The horse looked far superior to its rivals.
4. It had previously shown preference for the yielding ground prevalent that Friday.
5. The easy (in my opinion) Sandown 10 furlongs.

What more could you ask for?

Paddock inspection strengthened my opinion even more. The horse looked magnificent. Dick Hern was obviously thinking along the same lines as myself. I shopped around the bookies and eventually took 11/2, just missing a 6/1 offer by the skin of my teeth.

In the end things went my way, but only just — a photo-finish between Rhyme Royal and the favourite Le Soleil, a horse I have never fancied much, although he loves the soft ground. Willie Carson got home by a head from Brian Taylor, their mounts finishing 10 lengths in front of the rest of the field.

Stake	*Return*	*Actual Winnings*	*Bank (c/f £1,238)*
£50	£312	£262	£1,500

On the Saturday I did not back anything. There were no handicaps for the older horses. Marquee Universal, the Steve Cauthen Salisbury winner which had not impressed me, won the Esher Cup (40+) at 5/6.

Wed. May 2: The Victoria Cup at Ascot (45+). Always a great betting race. Run over the straight 7 furlongs, it is an important race for observations. Eighteen good handicappers turned out and again the ground was soft. I did not back anything. The straight course at Ascot is totally different from Sandown with its turns. There is no advantage here for the good class top-weighted horses and although there were a couple of possibilities, I was not convinced enough by anything to get any money down. The race eventually went to The Adrianstan at 25/1, a four-year-old ridden by Joe Mercer and trained by John Sutcliffe at Epsom. The horse came with a good late burst but I knew this one of old — brilliant on his day, but as often as not, totally unreliable. I did not note him down for the future.

One horse that did interest me a lot was Brian's Venture, the Newbury Spring Cup winner. He was ridden by Lester Piggott but had plenty to do with his 9 stone 4 lbs. Being at the top of the handicap at Ascot in the soft ground over the straight course is a decided disadvantage. The horse made a show for four furlongs and then predictably faded.

Thurs. Fri. Sat. May 3, 4, 5: The 'Guineas' meeting at Newmarket. One In a Million *did* win the 'Thousand' by the way — in great style at evens (1/1). I did not back it of course but the horse most certainly substantiated my theory about size. One In A Million had hardly a pick on her but boy could she accelerate. In one quick flash she left her high class rivals flat-footed.

Something I failed to mention earlier in regard to size is the fact that smaller, light framed, horses are much easier for a trainer to get to peak fitness than the massive gallopers. Some of those great lumps take ages to find form and need umpteen races to reach their best.

During the three days the only horses I noted down for the future was one that ran in the second race on the first day — Sea Chimes, trained by John Dunlop and ridden by the apprentice S. McCormack. This big handsome chestnut absolutely strolled away from its field in a modest 10 furlong apprentice handicap (0-60). It was the acceleration which impressed me. Any horse that can draw 4 lengths clear in the final furlong is well worth noting. While everyone left the course that day raving about One In A Million, I was convinced I had found a real good 'un in Sea Chimes. If I had only known at the time just how good he would turn out I would have doubled my bet every time he ran. However, that's what it's all about. Spotting, waiting, and then moving on cautiously.

APPENDIX

That first afternoon also showed up quite clearly the difference between my operation and other racing people's priorities. Sea Chimes' race was the one immediately before the Thousand Guineas and many chose to miss the apprentice race altogether in favour of viewing the classic contenders in the preliminary paddock. Well, because of pre-race publicity and conditioning they missed a real cracker. Sea Chimes remained unbeaten until July 1980 when he was the beaten favourite for the 'Eclipse' at Sandown, a Group One race for European champions. The would-be experts were taking note of him then all right. In terms of gambling though, it was while he was still a handicapper the money was to be made.

Mon. May 7: I decided to miss Kempton Park on the Monday and go to Doncaster instead since I strongly fancied Town and Country (Carson/Hern) in the Irish Sweeps Spring Handicap there (45+). I drove up early on Monday morning.

Town and Country had been one of my short list in 1978 and although he had a lot of weight to carry — 9 stone 9 lbs. — he was big, exceedingly brave, and had good quickening powers. Both Proven and Doogali were in opposition but I did not think of them as in the same class as my selection. He was on offer at around 4/1 and 5/1. I finally settled for 9/2.

The only thing that was bugging me was the softish ground and in the end this possibly brought defeat. Fluellen, an unpredictable mud-lover trained by Harry Wragg and ridden by Brian Taylor, won the race by ¾ length from Bertie Me Boy, a northern challenger, with Town And Country ½ length away third.

In bed in my hotel in the evening I mulled over the race again. Town and Country had looked great in the paddock, had every chance, and failed to quicken under Carson's strong driving. Doncaster is quite difficult right enough but he had won there in 1978 as well as York and Newbury and did not seem troubled by galloping tracks and the ground had not been that bad in the afternoon. The possibility that the five-year-old had finally been caught by the handicapper kept nagging at my mind. I said so to my companion beside me.

"They all look the same to me. Don't know one end from the other." Wanton, uneducated, harlot!

Stake	*Return*	*Actual Winnings*	*Bank (c/f £1,500)*
£50	Loser	None	£1,450

Tues. Wed. Thurs. May 8, 9, 10: I left Doncaster first thing and headed for Chester for the Spring Meeting. At this fixture my previous weeks of patience paid off handsomely.

On the first day Tesoro Mio was running. This was my winter favourite for collecting money in the coming season. I had been so impressed by this little horse in some of his 1978 victories that he was right at the top of my list of flyers. I reckoned that his turn of finishing speed was unequalled in the whole of British handicap racing. You may think I'm exaggerating but I actually predicted the race he would be aimed for. Round about January I sat down and worked out all the possibilities for

Tesoro Mio for the new season. I came up with the Ladbroke Chester Handicap (30-75) over 10 furlongs 85 yards for the older horses. The old formula again — a good accelerating animal on a sharp track. I mentioned my prediction to some friends in a discussion of the coming season. 'What the hell are you on about?' they said amidst their corn-ridden 'Guineas' and Derby prattling.

You can imagine my enthusiasm as I headed for Chester that day. And something else! Black Minstrel was out in the last race, a 7 furlong 122 yards handicap (0-70). Willie Carson was booked for the ride. This is the kind of day the flat racing handicap gambler dreams about all winter.

As far as I could see there wasn't a Satanist in sight. I felt a million dollars as I strolled through the old town among the throng.

The ground was soft. Black Minstrel would have no problems and Tesoro was perfectly at home on any ground. Everything looked right — one hundred per cent right.

When I saw Tesoro Mio in the paddock I knew I was on a good thing. He was alert, on the ball, and raring to go. Johnnie Seagrave, the Northern-based jockey, had to hold him in tightly on the way to the post. As usual, the track was absolutely mobbed and it is quite a fight from the paddock, situated in the middle of the course, to Tattersalls. When I finally arrived at the betting area I was astonished at the price of my horse — 9/1. On one bookie's board there was 10/1 for a brief moment. This, my friends, is the kind of situation where you have to have the courage of your convictions. What an extraordinary price! Everyone seemed to be going for the favourite Celebrated — the top-weight by the way, carrying 10 stone and ridden by Lester Piggott. In any other circumstances bar the presence of Tesoro Mio I would have backed Celebrated. The favourite's price shortened from 5/1 to 3's.

Very few horses enter the two furlong straight last at Chester and still win. This is exactly what Tesoro Mio did. The little colt, under 9 stone, absolutely mowed his rivals down to win in a photo-finish from Steve Cauthen on Neparree. Celebrated and Piggott were also in the photo a head away in third. I was delighted of course but at one point, even I thought Johnny Seagrave had left it a bit late. It just shows you how much of an advantage a backer has following horses with a good turn of foot.

Stake	*Return*	*Actual Winnings*	*Bank (c/f £1,450)*
£50	£480	£430	£1,880

I blundered a bit with Black Minstrel. I later learned he had opened up at 3/1 but by the time I reached the bookies from the paddock 2/1 was the best price available. 7/4 was the eventual starting price. One thing gnawing at me was Lester Piggott on the top-weight Casino Boy. As I mentioned earlier I had had a good win off this one a couple of years earlier when again under top weight. However, he had been sold out of Ryan Price's stable to Fred Rimmel for jumping purposes and when Ryan disposes of a horse you can bet your boots he has had, as far as flat racing handicapping is concerned, every inch of improvement out of him. I stuck with Black Minstrel.

Although he was rather slowly away, my selection improved throughout the straight and when Willie Carson urged him on, he sprinted clear inside the final furlong to win by a convincing 1½ lengths.

A very satisfactory day.

Stake	*Return*	*Actual Winnings*	*Bank (c/f £1,880)*
£50	£144	£94	£1,974

On Wednesday I was faced with quite a dilemma — in fact, a classic problem in the world of horse race gambling; would Lohengrin stay two furlongs more than he had in his Kempton Park victory. He was running in a three-year-old 10 furlong handicap (0-70).

On breeding there was no doubt that he would. His sire Rheingold was a close second in the 1972 Derby and his dam's sire Sea Bird II actually won the race in 1962. His dam was a reasonable performer around the mile mark. Nevertheless, in terms of acceleration, the distance question in racing is one of the most crucial. At the track when I reached the bookies he was on offer at evens (1/1). This more than anything made me decide to pass him over. I don't like the idea of laying out £50 to win £50 less tax — an actual profit margin of £46. It was only a four runner field right enough and I suppose many would argue that the price was reasonable, but I always believe that if you do not feel right over a bet then you must hold back. I did.

Lohengrin won by a comfortable 2 lengths.

On the Thursday I did not fancy anything and none of the winners impressed me. I had a really good drink at night in the hotel and headed for London first thing in the morning. The Friday card at Lingfield did not offer any races over my favoured distances.

Sat. May 12: The going at Lingfield on Saturday was heavy and the meeting took place in the morning and early afternoon to facilitate people wanting to watch the FA Cup Final on television. I was more interested in Black Minstrel. He was out for the 7 furlong 140 yards handicap (0-60) down there. Taking into account the race being run over the straight course, I thought he could win again. His victory at Chester had been very easy and again the ground was to his liking. I managed to get 7/2 which I thought was extremely generous. He finished at 11/4 favourite.

This time he was just held in a photo-finish by the aptly named Unexpected, a 16/1 bottom-of-the-handicap outsider ridden, ironically, by young Walter Swinburn. There was only a head in it at the line.

I felt I had been a bit unlucky and at first tended to blame Paul Cook, the jockey. The first two finished 4 lengths ahead of the rest of the field and it seemed to me he had misjudged his finishing run a bit. Later in the day, however, I veered more towards the theory that Black Minstrel had been brought out too soon after the Chester race.

Stake	*Return*	*Actual Winnings*	*Bank (c/f £1,974)*
£50	Loser	None	£1,924

I decided, since I had been on the go for over a month, to have a rest the next week. None of the Southern meetings at Windsor, Folkestone, or Brighton, had much to offer and my main activity was to record the York meeting on the video which I studied closely each night. There were a couple of interesting races on the tape but I did not note anything for a future bet.

As I have said repeatedly before, there's no need to be plunging in with your money every day. Although you cannot gauge it by the bank, a good rest is very profitable and much better for the morale than getting involved with foolish side bets based on nothing more than passing fancy.

Fri. Sat. May 18, 19: At the weekend I had the choice of Newbury or Newmarket. Without a doubt I chose Newmarket where a couple of my list were running. On the Saturday at Newbury Rhyme Royal, the 11/8 favourite, won the London Gold Cup (0-70) over 11 furlongs. Lester Piggott was on board but because of the short margin of the Sandown victory I passed him over. I thought he might just have been stopped by the weight on the long Newbury straight.

I went to Newmarket on Friday specifically to back House Guard ridden by Lester Piggott and trained at Newmarket by his brother-in-law Robert Armstrong. This horse had impressed me greatly in a couple of his 1978 victories. He was one of my leading fancies to improve further and win races in 1979. House Guard had already had an outing in a minor race at Pontefract on soft ground which does not really suit him. Lester was the only jockey who seemed to win on him. Since he was again booked for the ride — and on firm ground — I decided to plunge in.

House Guard opened at 4/1, which I snapped up, and was backed out of sight down to 85/40 (just over 2/1). He was always favourite. Piggott held him up most skilfully for a late burst just inside the final furlong. No bother at all.

I had a couple of bottles of Bollinger in Cambridge that night but refused an invitation to a party. It was the black leather and whip brigade again. I must admit I've formed a very sordid opinion of our upper seats of learning.

Stake	*Return*	*Actual Winnings*	*Bank (c/f £1,924)*
£50	£240	£190	£2,114 (double up time)

On Saturday I was all ready for the re-appearance of Sea Chimes in the 10 furlong three-year-old handicap (0-70). Although Red Rufus was in opposition I did not consider him as good a horse as Sea Chimes. I had now reached the stage of doubling up to £100 bets. I was hoping for a win. I took 5/2. Red Rufus was evens favourite after being backed from 2/1.

Sea Chimes, well ridden by George Duffield, improved to lead inside the final furlong and quickened away well to win by 2 lengths from Red Rufus. Eight ran.

More champagne at night and then home very contented indeed.

Stake	*Return*	*Actual Winnings*	*Bank (c/f £2,114)*
£100	£336	£236	£2,350

APPENDIX

Tues. Wed. Thurs. May 22, 23, 24: I went down and booked into an hotel at Chichester for the first Goodwood meeting of the year. It was a disappointing week altogether. I did not back a thing or see an animal for the notebook. Sometimes this happens and I'm afraid it's something you will just have to get used to. The expense can be heavy if you are having a lean time with your bets. But as I have said, it has value for future events if you can write off animals as one-paced or cowardly. This is the way you must think of such a week.

The evenings were a bit dull too except for the pansy who tried to get me back to his flat with him — an ex-naval man from Portsmouth I think he said he was.

Fri. Sat. May 25, 26: I motored up to Haydock early on Friday morning. I had decided to give Black Minstrel another go in the 7 furlong handicap there (30-75). The opposition seemed moderate and Willie Carson was again booked. The ground was still soft and I thought he was a bit of a good thing. I had taken the view that the big horse had been a bit unlucky at Lingfield. I was sure he could, with Carson's strength, pull off another victory before the ground firmed up.

I wish I had stayed at home. I managed to get a 3/1 bet about Black Minstrel but it mattered little in the end. Although Carson gave his all the horse failed to quicken in the final furlong. He finished a well beaten 4 length fourth. My apologies immediately went to Paul Cook. The horse had obviously come to the end of his little run of success. Either the handicapper had caught up with him or he had gone 'over the top' — a phrase used when a horse goes off the boil a bit and needs a break. I decided to drop him from the list for the time being. The one redeeming factor of the race was the style in which the winner, Judicial, won. Taffy Thomas brought him with a great run to win by only a short head. But, as always, it was his burst of speed which impressed me. He absolutely ploughed through the field at the finish. I took note of him immediately.

Stake	*Return*	*Actual Winnings*	*Bank (c/f £2,350)*
£100	Loser	None	£2,250

I stayed over at Liverpool for the evening and attended the Saturday meeting at Haydock. The rain had hit the South badly and the Windsor meeting was cancelled. I did not see anything particularly promising and came home to London directly after the meeting.

Mon. Tues. May 28, 29: Off to my local Sandown as fresh as paint on Monday morning. I saw an ideal chance to pick up cash. Brians Venture, the Newbury Spring Cup winner, was the 10 stone top-weight for the mile Whitsun Cup (40+). Lester Piggott was on board and the ground was on the soft side — the conditions which always favoured the horse. I picked up the extremely generous price of 13/2 and climbed up into the stands in anticipation.

Piggott was at his most masterful getting the horse home by a short head from the gutsy Smartset ridden by John Reid. It was a close thing but again my Sandown theories had been vindicated. A nice little win that was. Piggott actually got another top-weight home that day in the 14 furlong Richmond Handicap (0-70) with Marzook, trained by the crafty Jeremy Tree. However, it was outside my distance limits and I naturally let it pass.

Stake	*Return*	*Actual Winnings*	*Bank (c/f £2,250)*
£100	£720	£620	£2,870

On the Tuesday there was little of interest for me at the Sandown fixture. At Brighton later in the week the ground was soft and the card uninspiring. I give it a miss and concentrated on getting my notes and finances up to date.

Can you now see the logic behind my operation? Being only interested in a certain distance of race gives you lots of time to plan things out. Do not compare yourself to the big bookmaking firms who cover all the races all of the time. As with any other present-day business outfit, they have all sorts of accountants, lawyers, form experts, and computers, working for them.

By the end of May I had, since the beginning of the season, bet on only ten races (7 winners and 3 losers) and my cash was less than £200 away from trebling. At any given time I was in an excellent position to cushion any unlucky losses and there was no panic or worry involved in my gambling operation. Compare this to the high street idiot who bets on any old thing, regularly having about ten bets a day. He may have the occasional purple patch but in the end he's on to a hiding. It is physically and mentally impossible to make money his way.

Also worth mentioning at this point is the general mood of the racing press in springtime. Day and daily there are endless writings and theories on the forthcoming Derby and Oaks at Epsom in early June. It always seems at that time of year that all other Turf matters are of only minor importance. As far as you are concerned, let them all rave on. In fact, the more they do the less they will concentrate on our life-line, the handicaps. Do not be caught up in all the reports of thousands being heaped on to certain Derby runners. Even when these reports are true, the gamblers involved are, as often as not, embarking on some suicidal ego trip solely to impress their millionaire business contemporaries. These people have more money than they know what to do with and are not real professionals. Luckily for them, they do not depend on their bets to survive.

You will be subjected to this nonsense each April and May. Ignore the whole lot of it.

I must add that up to the Brians Venture gamble I had spent around £500 in petrol, fares, hotel bills, entrance money, booze, meals, sporting publications, and (hmph!) 'other extras'.

Wed. Thurs. Fri. Sat. June 6, 7, 8, 9: To be honest, the 1979 Derby Day was a disaster for me. Off I went dressed up like a dandy with high hopes of adding considerably to the bank. I held the opinion that Tesoro Mio was a certainty for the Daily Mirror

Handicap (40+) over 10 furlongs. Paul Cook had the ride and as far as I could see, none of the top-weights had much to offer in the way of acceleration. Tesoro is the small nippy type and having earlier romped home at Chester, I thought he would have no difficulty negotiating the tricky bends and cambers of Epsom.

In the Craven Handicap (35+) over 7 furlongs later in the afternoon, Lester Piggott was again booked for House Guard, second top-weight with 9 stone 10 lbs. including a 6 lbs. penalty for his Newmarket victory. I thought he too was unbeatable.

Well, as I say, it was one of those days when nothing goes right. Tesoro Mio, the 3/1 favourite from 5's did not come down the hill to Tattenham Corner at all well and it was only by the time the horses met the rising ground near the finish that he really got going. He finished about 6 lengths fourth to the front-running Philodantes, ridden by Steve Cauthen, trained by Barry Hills, and owned by 'Timeform' chief, Phil Bull. Timeform top-rated the 10/1 winner by the way.

We all have our day, us racing pro's. That Wednesday certainly wasn't mine.

Stake	*Return*	*Actual Winnings*	*Bank (c/f £2,870)*
£100	Loser	None	£2,770

Troy flew away with the Derby in great fashion showing the kind of burst I had been expecting from Tesoro Mio.

House Guard did not negotiate the track well either and Piggott had a difficult time with him. He finished a well beaten sixth to Red Johnnie, an Eddie Hide/Clive Brittain animal.

Stake	*Return*	*Actual Winnings*	*Bank (c/f £2,770)*
£100	Loser	None	£2,670

Thursday's meeting was abandoned because of a freak thunder storm. I've never known that to happen before at Epsom. Apparently after the deluge the ground around Tattenham Corner was treacherous. There were many complaints from the public that racing should have gone on and I was more than a bit disappointed myself. Lohengrin was to have turned out for the 12 furlong handicap (35-75). He was top-weight with Carson aboard. I really fancied him and was going to have a plunge. Instead I returned home and played the Wednesday races over on the video. I did some cursing that afternoon I can assure you. However, later in the evening I had a couple of cocktails and a good laugh over it. This is the way it must be. No sense lingering over past misfortune. You must move on.

On Friday, Sea Chimes, ridden by Willie Carson led all the way to win the 10 furlong Sun Life of Canada Handicap (0-65) at the generous price of 5/1 joint favourite. It was a good performance and, after the Wednesday débâcle, one which I was very grateful for.

Stake	*Return*	*Actual Winnings*	*Bank (c/f £2,670)*
£100	£576	£476	£3,146

There was nothing doing for me on the Saturday, again at Epsom.

June 11-June 18: Although I visited Lingfield, Newbury, and Sandown, during the next week or so, I saw little of interest for future betting. You sometimes find this in racing; a short lull between the major venues. The period between the Epsom Derby Meeting and Royal Ascot regularly falls flat and you find a whole load of mediocre races filling the cards at the meetings in between. By the time June comes around most trainers know the strengths and weaknesses of their various strings. They know the horses that have not lived up to expectations and they also have a good idea what animals are a few jumps ahead of the handicappers. The good progressive animals are either aimed at Royal Ascot itself or rested with some future big money event in mind. None of my listed horses appeared during this quiet period although Brians Venture (6/1) won again at York carrying Lester Piggott and top weight of 9 stone 6 lbs. The horse was not really one of my special flyers though. I had only backed him at Sandown because of the circumstances prevalent that day (top-weight + Lester + turning track). I naturally let the York event go and in the end Piggott was a bit lucky, being awarded the race in the Stewards' room after finishing second.

Tues. Wed. Thurs. Fri. June 19, 20, 21, 22: Royal Ascot is unquestionably a tremendous feast of racing, but there are many pitfalls at the meeting for the would-be gambler. On the first day, for example, there are no handicaps at all over our distances and the racing is better viewed with the future in mind rather than as a betting proposition. The only handicap of the day, the Ascot Stakes, over two and a half miles, was won by the 14/1 outsider Mons Beau, a fact that made me more than happy to be attending solely for paddock observations and eyeing up the crumpet.

Incidentally, the racecourse pantomime I mentioned earlier is at its most ridiculous during Royal Ascot Week. You've never seen such a collection of pains in the neck in your life. Many arrive with only one purpose in mind — showing off. And the lengths they go to do it sometimes verges on insanity. If some of the clothes on view were worn somewhere else, their owners would be locked up. For these idiots the horses are of only minor importance. It is merely another gathering in the social calendar.

The Wednesday meeting is a different story entirely as far as we are concerned. The Royal Hunt Cup (40+) over a mile, and the Bessborough Handicap (45+) over 12 furlongs, are of vital importance to us and, as often as not, throw up winners that have been held back for Royal Ascot and can win again afterwards. 1979 was no exception.

In the Hunt Cup, House Guard was again out but Lester Piggott had passed him over to ride the Lincoln winner Fair Season. I took the hint and did not back anything in the race. The eventual winner Pipedreamer, ridden by Philip Waldron and trained by Henry Candy, went straight into my notebook. I decided there and then to back him whenever he ran next. What a turn of speed! The best I had seen from a handicapper for a long time. He was held up most skilfully by Philip Waldron and then sailed through his field to produce that electrifying burst inside the last furlong. I had always regarded Pipedreamer more as a sprinting type before. However, once a horse wins a 24 runner Royal Hunt Cup over the Ascot straight mile, he can be defined quite categorically as a miler. A truly great performance and the type of horse tailor-made for our plans. The Bessborough winner also produced a nice turn of foot and he too went straight into the notebook — St. Briavels, a five-year-old horse ridden by John Reid and trained by Gavin Pritchard-Gordon at Newmarket.

By the way, horses are termed thus:

Colt: a male up to the age of four.
Horse: a male aged five or over.
Filly: a female up to the age of four.
Mare: a female aged five and over.
Gelding: a castrated horse.

On the Thursday I was faced with that same old problem again; would Sea Chimes stay another two furlongs, for Lester Piggott this time, in the 12 furlong King George V Stakes (45+)? I took the view that he may not. His sire Gulf Pearl normally produces horses that win around the mile mark — that was reasonable enough. But on his dam's side there was a strong strain of sprinting blood. His dam's sire St. Alphage is well known for producing six furlong sprinters.

It was a near thing though. The horse had easily won over a mile and a quarter and looked as if he would stay the extra distance. And with the assistance of Lester too — maybe I should have plunged in. I certainly thought so after the race. Piggott had his mount in the leading group throughout and gave him the go-ahead two furlongs out. Sea Chimes, the 3/1 favourite, responded in grand style and quickened away to win by no less than 6 lengths. So much for my breeding theories!

On Friday the Britannia Handicap (35+) for three-year-olds over the Royal Hunt Cup mile, produced another flyer in Welsh Chanter, ridden by Joe Mercer and trained by Henry Cecil. The colt came with a tremendous run and strode clear in the final furlong to win by 2 lengths. Into the files he went, but unfortunately he did not appear again for the rest of the season. As it turned out, Sea Chimes had made *his* last appearance for the year too.

Sat. June 23: On the Saturday of the Royal Ascot Week they have what is known as the 'Ascot Heath' Meeting. It is really just a continuation of the Royal Meeting minus all the poseurs and swankers.

That day I noted an impressive filly in the mile handicap (30-75) for three-year-old fillies over the straight course — Strathspey, ridden by Greville Starkey and trained by Ian Balding. I liked the way the horse pulled right away from her field to win by 3 lengths. It was a very creditable victory because the second horse, Rectitude, had won an important £7,000 handicap at the Derby Meeting only a fortnight earlier. I noted Strathspey down as one well worth watching for in the near future.

I did not note anything in the big £7,500 Andy Capp Handicap (35+) run over 10 furlongs at Redcar the same afternoon. I watched the race on the video at night over a few whiskies. It was a multiple photo-finish with a neck, a short head, half a length, a neck, and a neck, separating the first six horses. Nothing outstanding there, although the winner, Side Track, won the same race again in 1980. Chalet, the 4 length Newmarket winner was in the race with top weight. But he was jumping from seven to ten furlongs and I did not take a chance with him. It was a good decision. The horse ran well until about a mile out then faded badly to finish well down the field — second last of 13 as a matter of fact.

As you will have noticed, I did not bet at all during Royal Ascot although I was only a kick in the shirt off it with Sea Chimes. But at the end of the five days I was a happy man. I was well armed for the 'high summer' ahead with a few good additional flyers in the notebook. Many people take the view that because of all the ballyhoo and publicity over an important meeting, it is imperative to involve themselves in the betting side of things. They feel left out if they don't. How can I stand aside and let all this activity fly past? they think.

As I have said before, only get the money down when you are good and ready. This is vitally important. Forget about the prestige of the meetings. A 5/1 winner at Edinburgh yields exactly the same profit as a 5/1 winner at Royal Ascot. Keep cool friends, and train yourself to lie low if none of your horses are out.

Mon. Tues. June 25, 26: Now that the ground had firmed up considerably, I decided to head down to Brighton for the early-week meeting there. I had a strong fancy that my top-weight turning track theory would pay dividends in the mile handicap (30-75) there. So Proper a Guy Harwood/Greville Starkey animal, winner of six races in 1978, was top-weight with 10 stone. Two of his previous victories had been at Epsom which, as you now know, is very similar to Brighton and I was of the opinion that he would go in again.

Starkey tried to make all on the 6/1 shot but was swamped in the last furlong by the six-year-old Andy Rew and Northleach, a John Dunlop four-year-old. Tough luck!

I stayed the night at Brighton and got exceedingly drunk. Around midnight I decided to go for a paddle to cool my feet down a bit. I had covered almost every bar in town by that time and between this and the day's racing, the old toes were on fire.

I got down to the beach and looked around for somewhere to put my shoes and socks. It was quite dark and I didn't want them to go missing the way my trousers did at Ayr that other night. I spotted an upturned rowing boat further down the shore. The very thing.

Along I crunched through the pebbles and stones. Just as I was about to sit down and take my shoes and socks off I heard this kind of grating sound coming from underneath the boat. Any other time I would have run for my life, but full of whisky and Carlsberg Specials there's none braver than your Stewart.

I heaved the boat up and there lying on an old tarpaulin were two Pakistani's, boy and girl, absolutely stark naked, in the most compromising of positions. She was on top of him as a matter of fact. Nothing at all was said between the three of us. I just gently put the boat back down and crunched off.

And all those stories you hear too — about what honourable people the Paki's and Indians are. It just shows you doesn't it?

Stake	*Return*	*Actual Winnings*	*Bank (c/f £3,146)*
£100	Loser	None	£3,046

I visited the course (Brighton) for the next day's meeting but the horses were a moderate lot and I neither backed nor noted anything.

Wed. Thur. June 27, 28: On Wednesday I went down to Salisbury. There were a couple of good handicaps on offer, and with the ground now firm all over the South, they were not to be missed. In the Bilbury Cup (30-75) for three-year-olds over 12 furlongs, I was very impressed by Dick Hern's Lindoro ridden by Willie Carson. The colt quickened away in great fashion to win very easily by 3 lengths. I thought that day he was a sure future money-spinner.

In the 10 furlong Gwen Blagrave Memorial Handicap (35+) the winner Haul Knight put up a good performance to win by 4 lengths although he was in the lead from about two and a half furlongs out. Neither he nor any of his challengers quickened at all. It is sometimes very hard to know exactly what to make of this kind of victory. You don't know whether to assume the horse has improved to the tune of his winning distance or has just managed to poach an unassailable lead at some point in the race. The Easter Roseberry Handicap winner, Proven, put up a brave effort to be second with 9 stone 11 lbs. The weight really tells up the straight at Salisbury and I would not blame any horse for faltering there with such a burden.

On the Thursday Portese put up a fine performance in the mile handicap (0-70) to win under 9 stone 13 lbs. I did not note him however, because of the poor quality of his rivals.

Fri. Sat. June 29, 30: To be quite honest with you I was absolutely exhausted come Friday of that week. I had been on the go non-stop since the Tuesday of Royal Ascot and the train journey back from Salisbury on Thursday night really got on my nerves. I fell out with an old bitch with two stupid red-ribboned poodles, one of which knocked over my expensive British Rail double whisky.

When this type of thing happens you must recognise and diagnose the signs immediately. I needed a break. In fact, it does more harm than good continuing in such a mood. I gave Lingfield and Newmarket a miss over the weekend, did some gardening (weeding actually), and recorded the TV racing.

Wed. Thurs. July 4, 5: Off down to Brighton again. The Monday and Tuesday meetings at Windsor and Folkestone had little to offer and by the time Wednesday came I was raring to go. I had a lovely seafood lunch in a restaurant in the morning then up to Race Hill for the meeting.

The card was not spectacular but I made a special note of Northleach, a John Dunlop/Willie Carson animal. The colt only won by half a length right enough but, after not having much room coming up the straight, he fairly flew home in the final furlong. It was a great burst of acceleration and I felt sure he would win again soon. I had, as you know, seen the horse at the previous Brighton meeting when he was second in So Proper's race. I had not been over impressed by him that day. However, there was talk around that the virus had hit some of John Dunlop's horses and Northleach was obviously just returning to his best, having won earlier on in the season and then showing a dramatic loss of form.

The Thursday did not throw up anything worth noting. By the way, just as a matter of interest I visited the old rowing boat again late on the Wednesday night. There was no activity underneath except for a couple of crabs fighting with each other. My 'friend' and I evicted them and moved in.

Fri. Sat. July 6, 7: I did not fancy anything at Sandown on the Friday but Saturday's racing presented me with a right old headache. St. Briavels, the Royal Ascot winner, was out in the Old Newton Handicap (40+), an £11,000 mile and a half event at Haydock and Judicial, the horse that had impressed me greatly when beating Black Minstrel, was entered in the Victoria Handicap (0-60) over 7 furlongs at Sandown. To make matters even worse, I had a notion that Red Johnnie, House Guard's Epsom conqueror could utilise my turning track theory. He was second top-weight in the Judicial race with Piggot aboard. He was, in my book, the 'real' top-weight. The eight-year-old Nearly New, the only horse above Red Johnnie in the handicap, was only carrying his heavy burden because of past achievements for which he had never been let off the hook and was unlikely to equal again.

What should I do?

Because of the competitive field and predictable open betting in the Sandown event, I split my stake between Judicial and Red Johnnie. I instructed, with the promise of a good backhander, a trusted friend to nip down to Sandown and place the bets. Then, early on Saturday morning, I drove to Haydock and plunged in on St. Briavels at the outrageously generous price of 7/1.

What a day it turned out to be!

St. Briavels, carrying a 7 lb. penalty, did exactly as he had done at Ascot, coming with a grand rattle at the finish under the skilfull driving of John Reid to squeeze through and win by a length. Judicial, at 8/1 with Paul Cook aboard, also came with a strong late burst to snatch the spoils at Sandown. There was only a neck in it. Red Johnnie was a disappointing sixth at 9/2. Have a look at the bank now after those weeks of patience.

Stake (St. Briavels)	*Return*	*Actual Winnings*	*Bank (c/f £3,046)*
£100	£768	£668	£3,714

Stake (Judicial & Red Johnnie)	*Return*	*Actual Winnings*	*Bank (c/f £3.174)*
£100	£432 (£50)	£332	£4,046 (double up time)

APPENDIX

Tues. Wed. Thurs. July 10, 11, 12: I got up to Newmarket like a shot on the Tuesday for the first July Meeting on the July Course. Pipedreamer was out for the Ward Hill Bunbury Cup (35+), a straight 7 furlong handicap worth around £7,400. As Pipedreamer had already won over Ascot's straight mile, I saw no problems at all for him on the course. House Guard was in the race but once again Piggott had passed him over. His eventual 20/1 price confirmed further that he wasn't fancied all that much. Quite frankly I thought Pipedreamer was a certainty. And I wasn't the only one. I learned later that someone had pulled off a spectacular £16,000 to £2,000 on him. I myself got £1,600 to £200 (8/1), the bank now indicating a double up.

Philip Waldron again held the horse up. When given a little slap he bolted through the field to win going away by 2 lengths.

Stake	*Return*	*Actual Winnings*	*Bank (c/f £4,046)*
£200	£1,728	£1,528	£5,574

On the Wednesday Strathspey, ridden by Lester Piggott, was out for the 7 furlong Duchess of Montrose Handicap (35+) for three-year-old fillies. She won all right but because of the odds-on prices available (around 4/5-4/6) I did not bet. I have never been happy with odds-on shots although I could have cleared around £140 for my £200 bet.

It just seems to be inherent in me not to lay out more money than I will actually win in the end. The theory was well substantiated in the next race — the 10 furlong Duke of Cambridge Handicap (30-75) for three-year-olds.

Lindoro, the impressive Salisbury winner, went for the race and although the event was two furlongs shorter than at Salisbury, I thought he was a good thing, taking into account the long difficult mile straight at Newmarket. He was odds-on (10/11) by the time I arrived at the bookies. I let him go too.

To be honest, it looked as if Willie Carson made a right mess of the ride, getting badly boxed in a couple of times when the field entered the last two furlongs. The horse finished like an express but was beaten a neck by Born To Reason, a Ryan Price trained animal ridden by Brian Taylor. He should never have been beaten. However, in subsequent events Lindoro proved himself to be a bit of a handful and was eventually scratched from my own personal list which, I suppose, exonerates Willie considerably for the defeat.

Bad luck aside, supposing I had backed those two odds-on shots. At the end of the day after a winner and a loser, I would have lost money after paying the betting tax. In my opinion this is no way to gamble for profit.

The Thursday was a good enough day's racing but contained nothing for me betting-wise or for the files.

Fri. Sat. July 13, 14: At the weekend I fancied a couple of top-weights at Chester but again the prices were unattractive — they both won by the way — one of them being Chalet, again reverting to his Newmarket winning distance of 7 furlongs.

Without any hesitation I headed North that weekend, for York. I did not arrive until late on the Friday night and missed the afternoon meeting. But it was the Saturday afternoon I was concerned with. Tesoro Mio was out for the John Smiths

Magnet Cup (40+) over 10 furlongs 110 yds. — one of my favourite races of the year. I was a bit afraid of Town And Country but really could not see past Tesoro. I still held the opinion that he was way out in front of the handicappers, and with his finishing turn of foot I had the outcome of the race already pictured in my mind before the event took place.

I got 8/1 and the race went like clockwork. Eddie Hide held up Tesoro Mio in the usual way, improved throughout the straight, and sprinted away when asked for his effort. He won by a comfortable 2½ lengths with Town And Country a brave second under 10 stone. A great victory (for me).

Stake	*Return*	*Actual Winnings*	*Bank (c/f £5,574)*
£200	£1,728	£1,528	£7,102

I baled out of York the minute I collected my bets (4 @ £50) and drove back to London. In anticipation of victory I had a few guests invited for later in the evening. I consumed four bottles of 'Moet' that night and ended up whooping it up to Jimmy Shand records out on the lawn. None of the dogs in the area seemed to appreciate it. Some of them became quite hysterical and barked all night. (I was told when I wakened later the next day — much later!)

Tues. July 17: I set out for Folkestone on the Tuesday specifically to back Yellow Rock, a Guy Harwood three-year-old ridden by Greville Starkey. I had noted the animal in 1978 as one likely to improve. It was the old top-weight strategy again. The horse was set to carry 9 stone 7 lbs., a full 13 lbs. heavier than its nearest rival. As I mentioned before, I like this kind of set-up — an animal far superior to its rivals on a tight track. The race (0-55) was over 7 furlongs and close paddock inspection only convinced me further to have a plunge. The opening price was 9/2 but after my bets and some others, 3/1 was all that could be had at the 'off' — or what should have been the 'off'. Brian Taylor's mount, Brave Connection, decided to live up to her name and had a boot at Yellow Rock after they were installed. Yellow Rock then reared up and backed out of the stalls, half killing Starkey in the process. Both horses ended up out at the back of the stalls and the starter allowed the rest of the field to gallop off without them. As the start of the race was on the far side of the track, there was much confusion in the stands whether the pair had come under starters orders or not — a vital point in this kind of situation.

When the horses in a race are all loaded up in the stalls, a white flag is raised by the starter's assistant and from then on, as far as betting is concerned, your horse is deemed a 'runner', even if it gets left at the start. If any incident, such as I have described above, happens before the white flag goes up and a horse is left, then it becomes a 'non-runner' and your stake is returnable.

Unfortunately for me, and many others, Yellow Rock and Brave Connection *had* come under orders. I lost my cash without even getting a run for it. Naturally the bookies were delighted. I cursed all the way back to London.

Stake	*Return*	*Actual Winnings*	*Bank (c/f £7,102)*
£200	Loser	None	£6,902

Wed. Thurs. July 18, 19: Both the Kempton fixtures were in the evening. Nothing much happened on the Wednesday except for the bloke who tried to start a fight with me because I stood on his toe — cheeky swine he was! I made a big show of being held back by another racegoer. I'm not a fighting man of any sorts; kind of cowardly I would say — yes, definitely a coward.

On Thursday night House Guard, this time with Piggott back on board, went for the mile Mortlake Handicap (0-60). He was top-weight with 10 stone. The ground was really firm now and, without doubt, he looked a good thing. I took 5/2, just missing an 11/4 offer which was hastily rubbed out after a rush of money. Obviously I wasn't the only one there to collect.

Piggott rode a masterly race, holding the colt up until the last second before quickening in great style to win by an easy ¾ length. No bother at all — like taking candy from a bookie!

Stake	*Return*	*Actual Winnings*	*Bank (c/f £6,902)*
£200	£672	£472	£7,374

Sat. July 21: On Friday night I motored up to Scotland for Saturday's meeting at Ayr. Northleach, the impressive Brighton winner was out for a 7 furlong handicap (0-55) there. When John Dunlop sends a horse all the way from Arundel down in Sussex up to Scotland, it's time to sit up and take note. John Reid was booked for the ride. It looked a good set-up.

In the paddock Northleach looked terrific and I thought the 9/2 which I snapped up, extremely generous. As at Brighton, the horse made good headway in the straight and burst through in the last few yards to win by a neck. It was close but never really in any doubt.

Stake	*Return*	*Actual Winnings*	*Bank (c/f £7,374)*
£200	£1,056	£856	£8,230 (double up time)

That same Saturday the elusive Chalet was out again but this time over the straight Newmarket mile (50+). Because of the stamina question which hung over him I was not sure he would get the distance. His previous victory, if you remember, had been over the easy Chester 7 furlongs 122 yds. I again passed him over. He again won, at 13/8. He did not appear again for the rest of the season. Between low prices and distance questions I just could not pin that horse down at all. And he had been in the notebook since April too.

Also that same afternoon my old friend Tesoro Mio was out for the Ripon Bell-Ringer Handicap (30/75) over his favourite 10 furlongs. For his big York victory he had an 8 lbs. penalty. Even with that I thought he was an absolute certainty. In the press he was quoted at evens (1/1) favourite in the six runner field. I was of the opinion he would eventually start odds-on at around 4/6. Even for Tesoro I had no intention of entertaining odds like that.

Well, as it turned out, I got that race completely wrong. The horse ended up at evens and was beaten 1½ lengths by Marquee Universal, the beginning-of-the-season Salisbury winner. Quite frankly I could not believe it when I heard the result. I was damned lucky the field and starting price hadn't been bigger. In those circumstances I would have definitely have gone to Ripon, backing Northleach in a high street shop there. I heard later that Tesoro Mio had fitness problems, but being only a week after his magnificent York triumph, I still find this form inexplicable — even yet.

Wed. Thurs. July 25, 26: I got back from Scotland late on Sunday night, exhausted and dying with a hangover. I laid low until the Wednesday evening meeting at Sandown.

In the mile handicap (0-60), House Guard and Lester Piggott again. The horse accelerated inside the furlong to beat Greenhill God by a short head. From 11/2 to 3's he went. I got 5/1 just before the rush started. The winner and the second were the two top-weights. Greenhill with 10 stone and House Guard with 10 stone 13 lbs. The next heaviest horse had 8 stone 10 lbs.

Can you see the pattern now? You'll be out there pitching soon yourself.

Stake	*Return*	*Actual Winnings*	*Bank (c/f £8,230)*
£400	£2,304	£1,904	£10,134

In the next race, the Playboy Bookmakers Handicap (0-65) over 10 furlongs, I was not surprised to see second top-weight Red Rufus take the spoils. However, there was a case to be made for a few in that event and I left him alone. He was returned at 7/1 with, at one point, 8's available. It would have been a good bet.

The Sandown Thursday afternoon meeting saw a continuance of the Yellow Rock pantomime. In the 7 furlong Bow Street Handicap (0-60) I thought he had a good chance of winning. The opposition was very weak and as I said earlier, the horse had impressed me quite a bit in 1978 and was particularly suited to the firm ground.

Well, everything went according to plan. I picked up 6/1 and Starkey got him home by a head. The only trouble was, he hampered the second, Kalazero, in the process. After a stewards' inquiry he was disqualified and placed second. I was sick as two parrots. Not only had I lost my cash; the Sandown 'victory' more than verified that, had he taken part, he would undoubtedly have won at Folkestone. The winner of the Folkestone race, Heavenly Chorus, was back in fourth place.

And a £400 bet too — bastard!

Stake	*Return*	*Actual Winnings*	*Bank (c/f £10,134)*
£400	Loser	None	£9,734

APPENDIX

Fri. Sat. July 27, 28: I went to Ascot for the two days but nothing caught my eye — except Troy of course, winner of the Group One £94,000 King George VI and Queen Elizabeth Stakes. Not much of an investment though at 2/5.

Tues. Wed. Thurs. Fri. July 31, Aug. 1, 2, 3: Down to Chichester for the big Goodwood Meeting. I slipped up a bit on the very first race. Strathspey, ridden by Lester Piggott, was favourite for the 7 furlong Tapestry Handicap (35-75) and although I learned later that she had been around 2/1, the best available when I got round from the paddock was 11/10. I passed her over. She ended up at 13/8 and won the race by a head. Too bad! As with Chalet, I could not get a good bet out of this one either.

I did not have a bet until the Thursday when Northleach appeared again, this time for the mile Drayton Handicap (0-70). I thought he was a good thing. Willie Carson was booked for the ride. The horse opened in the market at 100/30. I helped myself to 3/1 as he advanced to 5/2 favourite. Carson brought him with a great rattle to win by a length.

Stake	*Return*	*Actual Winnings*	*Bank (c/f £9,734)*
£400	£1,536	£1,136	£10,870

On the Friday I thought, given a bit more room than at Newmarket, Lindoro could take the 10 furlong Extel Handicap (45+). He was advertised at around 5/2 by most firms in the morning press but at the track a barrowload of money was piled on him. I was lucky to get 2/1 before he dropped to 6/4 favourite.

As it turned out I was *dead* lucky that day. Lindoro was beaten ¾ length by Red Rufus but got the race by courtesy of the Goodwood Stewards who disqualified the winner for boring in towards Carson's mount. I was delighted with the outcome of course but I personally thought Pat Eddery and Red Rufus were very harshly treated, especially being placed last. They were, in my opinion, the winners on merit and Lindoro, in spite of Carson's frantic driving, seemed reluctant to go through with his effort when the chips were down. I scrubbed him from my list immediately.

Stake	*Return*	*Actual Winnings*	*Bank (c/f £10,870)*
£400	£1,152	£752	£11,622

That same night House Guard and Lester Piggott won at Newmarket over the straight mile (0-60). There was no way I could get there in time and I could not contact my trusted friend either — he was, in fact, off for a dirty weekend with some floosie he had picked up during his celebrations after backing Judicial himself. Good luck to him! But it was a shame. House Guard was backed from 2/1 to 6/4 favourite.

In fact, talking about Judicial, he was declared for Newmarket on the Saturday afternoon and, since I had no intention of missing *him* too, I got back up to London late on Friday night. None of my horses were out at the Saturday Goodwood meeting and as far as the top-weights were concerned, midweek rain had softened the ground a bit and substantially reduced their chances. My decision was a good one; none of the top-weights won.

Sat. July 4: As Judicial was running in the last race of the afternoon, I did not hurry getting myself to Newmarket. I stopped for a pub lunch (alcohol free) at Bishop's Stortford, a nice town about half way on the journey. I got to the course just as the first race was about to start — a two-year-old six furlong affair. The winner accelerated in great style. Not a bad sort, I thought to myself.

Racing's a funny old business for sure. That two-year-old winner, Quick as Lightning, went on to win the One Thousand Guineas in 1980.

Anyway, after taking 7/2 about Judicial (he finally finished at 9/4 favourite), Bruce Raymond brought him with a tremendous burst to win by a head. It was another close thing but, as I saw it, the horse won easily. As soon as he started his final surge the race was never in doubt.

When I say *he* about Judicial by the way, I am only partly correct. The horse is, in fact, a gelding. No doubt your interest has been fired by my earlier terminology — 'a castrated horse'. Well yes, it means exactly as you thought — a horse with his balls cut off. Sometimes when colts are so infatuated by the opposite sex that it effects their racing performance, it is deemed necessary to castrate them and relieve them of their plight. In many cases it works wonders, and from then on the horse concentrates solely on running fast — probably to get as far away from his trainer as possible. On other occasions it makes no difference whatsoever to the horse's race times — a rather unfortunate situation you might agree.

I've often thought that some of our trainers and jockeys would benefit greatly by a similar operation.

Stake	*Return*	*Actual Winnings*	*Bank (c/f £11,622)*
£400	£1,728	£1,328	£12,950

Tues. Wed. Thurs. Aug. 7, 8, 9: On the first day of the Brighton three day meeting I did not bet and nothing caught my eye. On the second day, the Wednesday, I took a right beating.

There was rain around but the ground was still reasonably good. Yellow Rock was top weight in the 7 furlong Ladbroke Betcha Handicap (0-55) and I thought this, at last, was his chance to put things right. After all, he still hadn't been beaten and as for my theories, he hadn't done anything to suggest he had lost any of his ability. He was also a course and distance winner, having won at Brighton in 1978. Things looked good. Greville Starkey was again aboard. He finished 4/1 favourite. I got 9/2 but it was all a waste of time. Yellow Rock finished tenth of thirteen and was immediately struck from my list.

Stake	*Return*	*Actual Winnings*	*Bank (c/f 12,950)*
£400	Loser	None	£12,550

In the next race the 12 furlong Brighton Challenge Cup Handicap (30-75), St. Briavels, the Royal Ascot and Haydock winner, was out. He too was top weight. Since his two victories he had gone over to Ostend for a £50,000 race there and was beaten, but I still thought he would be far too good for his other five Brighton rivals.

Another farce. John Reid brought him with his challenge about a furlong out but he found nothing and was beaten ¾, short head, ¾, into fourth. Countess Palotta, a Henry Candy/Philip Waldron front-runner, led the whole way to win the race. St. Briavels was a 3/1 chance.

Stake	*Return*	*Actual Winnings*	*Bank (c/f £12,550)*
£400	Loser	None	£12,150

There was more rain overnight and on Thursday the going was soft. I did not back anything. Possibly the ground had been slightly against Yellow Rock but I could not accept this as the sole answer for defeat. Third last of thirteen is no form to go forward with for the future, especially at an easy course such as Brighton. Predictably, in his subsequent three runs he still failed to win. Damned expensive animal that was for me.

As far as St. Briavels was concerned, he probably needed a rest after Ostend. He too ran another three times and failed to win. Luckily I left him alone. After all, he was a five-year-old, and continued improvement is very difficult at that age for a horse racing on the 'flat'. The official handicappers do not forget Royal Ascot victories in a hurry when allocating weight.

Sat. Aug. 11: My next meeting was at Redcar on the Saturday. I went up there to back Pipedreamer in the £12,000 William Hill Gold Cup (40+), a straight mile handicap.

It was one of those crazy racing days with meetings all over the place at Lingfield, Newmarket, Haydock, and, of course, Redcar. For me much decision making. Tesoro Mio was out at Newmarket in a mile and a half handicap. Because of the fitness question, the extra two furlongs, and the mysterious Ripon defeat, I gave him a miss. It was a good idea. He finished second last of eight and did not run again for the rest of the season, although he figured in the ante-post betting for the important Cambridgeshire Handicap at Newmarket later in the year.

Further complications cropped up with the gallant House Guard turning out at Haydock for a mile amateur riders handicap. I never touch horses ridden by amateurs — a good philosophy normally. House Guard won by ½ length at 7/1 — bastard!

After Royal Ascot and Newmarket the handicappers had shown little mercy with Pipedreamer, allotting him joint top weight with Portese, the Salisbury winner I referred to earlier.

Although it was a straight mile I was, because of the straight Royal Hunt Cup and Bunbury Cup victories, still confident. Pipedreamer's finishing burst would see him through. So I thought. He weakened about two furlongs out and finished seventh of the eleven runners. Possibly the weight was too much for him. He isn't that big by the way. However, it did not stop Portese. He won the race by ¾ length from Greenhill God, House Guard's Sandown rival.

As far as straight courses were concerned, Pipedreamer had been stopped by the handicappers. What a bloody week!

Stake	*Return*	*Actual Winnings*	*Bank (c/f £12,150)*
£400	Loser	None	£11,750

It was time for a little pick-me-up. A good opportunity turned up two races after the Pipedreamer catastrophe. I cheered home the winner like a madman — an 11/1 outsider called Delaneys Cross.

"Go on my beauty! go on my son! easy!" Into the bar after the race rubbing my hands in delight.

"Some folk have all the luck."

"Luck dear? Don't kid yourself."

"That donkey's done nothing all year."

"I know a wee bit about this game." (tapping my temple in typical inside information fashion).

"What are you talking about? it was only three quarters of a length."

"Inch is as good as a mile, fancy some champagne?"

"If you're buying."

"No bother, what's your name anyway?"

"Diane."

"Oh I like that. Listen Diane, how do you fancy . . ."

Wed. Aug. 15: Judicial's next engagement surprised me no end. 'He' turned out for a small, but quite competitive, 7 furlong handicap (0-65) at Catterick. Naturally he was near the top of the handicap, being rated around 50 at the time. On Catterick's tight circuit I thought he was a good thing. Remember, his last victory was at Newmarket. When a good accelerating animal drops from a Group One course to Group Four level you really are on to something.

I travelled over night and got up there early on Wednesday morning. I had a little nap in the car, breakfast in town, and set off for the track at lunch time. My big worry was that I would not get a decent price. He was 3/1 in the morning paper. If I could get that I'd be quite happy.

In the event, he opened up at 100/30 favourite (approx 3⅓/1) which I just missed. I eventually got my 3/1 in four separate bets. It is much more important to do this at the minor meetings. Occasionally, if a market is weak, bookmakers will refuse largish bets, only taking part of them and reducing the price immediately so that a mushrooming process develops and you end up with sadly reduced odds everywhere. But although Catterick is only Group Four, it does have quite a strong betting market owing to the big crowds that turn up there.

In argument, I would partly accept that I was a bit over-cautious about betting this way. I just automatically split up big bets into manageable and insignificant amounts. Many people who back in large sums use the same bookies all the time and get to know them as kind of friends. I have no wish for any such phoney relationships. It's all-out warfare as far as I'm concerned and, as I mentioned before, the same bookies think nothing of using all the tricks of the trade to fox their clients.

Judicial ended up as 11/4 favourite and won by a hairy short head. I think even Bruce Raymond, the jockey, would agree he left things very late indeed.

Stake	*Return*	*Actual Winnings*	*Bank (c/f £11,750)*
£400	£1,536	£1,136	£12,886

Fri. Aug. 17: On the Friday at Newbury Strathspey, the Goodwood winner I missed, stepped up a bit in class and went for the Hungerford Stakes, a Group Three event. Not being my territory I did not bet. She was a creditable fourth.

I was at the meeting to back the other Goodwood victor, Northleach, in the one mile Russley Handicap (0-70). The race was on the round course and I thought my selection's finishing burst would see him through. I got a generous 7/1. In the race Willie Carson found himself boxed in and after having his effort blocked off, Northleach couldn't quicken again. Few horses can accelerate twice in the short hectic last two furlongs of a race. He finished a well beaten seventh of twelve. Tough luck! Move on.

Stake	*Return*	*Actual Winnings*	*Bank (c/f £12,886)*
£400	Loser	None	£12,486

As August draws to an end it is time to be very discriminative in your betting. Some of the horses on your list will continue to win throughout the whole season, but others will become weary and need a break. My own betting operation gradually slows down at this time of year and you will notice the dates between my bets widening considerably. This is quite natural. You should have made the backbone of your bank by this time and just be coasting towards the end of the season. The straight tracks will now be out for many ~~of~~ your good handicappers because of the welter burdens of weight allotted them. The ones that still manage to win will be considered, by their trainers, too good for handicap racing. You will see many of them entering into Group Three and sometimes Group Two racing. At this time you must keep an eye open for betting opportunities on the turning tracks where the weight will not be too punishing for your flyers.

Tues. Wed. Thurs. Aug. 21, 22, 23: The big August York Meeting was an entertaining few days but nothing more than a holiday for me. There were no betting opportunities and I did not add anything to the notebook. In the circumstances, I may have stayed at home and viewed the meeting on television, but the major ITV strike of last year put paid to many video plans. I felt I had to attend in case some late-developing flyer was overlooked.

Mon. Tues. Aug. 27, 28: My next gambling operation was at the Epsom Bank Holiday Meeting. The ground was firm and I decided to look among the advantageous top-weighted handicappers for money-making.

Unfortunately I was not convinced by the abilities of McAdam, top-weight in the 12 furlong Cicero Handicap (0-60) to back him. It was a great pity. He won at 12/1.

In the Ranmore Handicap (0-65) over one mile 110 yds. the actual top-weight Steel Trade with 10 stone had never been one of my favourites while second top-weight Tender Heart with 9 stone 13 lbs. had, a couple of times, been on the verge of entering my notebook. The next heaviest in the race had only 8 stone 11 lbs., miles below Tender Heart in ability. I decided, after careful paddock inspection, to have a go.

Ex-jockey and now trainer, Geoff Lewis, brought Tender Heart with a well-timed run to win easily by 2½ lengths. In fact, the gelding, trained by John Sutcliffe at Epsom brought off one of the biggest gambles of modern times when he won the Royal Hunt Cup at Ascot in 1980. The betting involved then amounted to hundreds of thousands of pounds.

But at Epsom it was a good little win for me too considering previous recent losses. 6/1 I got.

Stake	*Return*	*Actual Winnings*	*Bank (c/f £12,486)*
£400	£2,688	£2,288	£14,774

On the Tuesday I went for Palemon at 10/1 carrying 9 stone 13 lbs. in the 10 furlong PTS Harlequin Handicap (0-65) despite having some doubt about the suitability of the course for him. He is a muscular and rather heavy colt, but I thought he was so superior to his rivals, his ability would see him through. It didn't! He finished last of eight. The camber in the straight was just too tricky for him and all Bruce Raymond could do was ease him right up in the closing stages of the race.

Stake	*Return*	*Actual Winnings*	*Bank (c/f £14,774)*
£400	Loser	None	£14,374

Sat. Sept. 1: On the Saturday at Sandown was what I considered the best bet of the whole of last season. In the mile William Hill Handicap (30-75) Pipedreamer was allotted top weight with 10 stone. The ground was firm, the course easy. Tender Heart and Brians Venture were also in the race but there was just no way I could see past Pipedreamer. I thought he was an absolute certainty. Paddock inspection only strengthened my opinion more. He looked great in the warm sunshine.

Now, even if after reading this book you aren't too keen on my methods, I am sure you would still concede that I do know a bit about the game. And if I told you I thought a horse was a certainty and possibly one of the best bets around for years, I'm sure you would at least consider it seriously, wouldn't you?

Taking this into consideration you would then, I assume, come to the conclusion that many others in the racing world would also recognise what an outstanding chance Pipedreamer had and that he would be widely tipped and low in the betting. Well, take note carefully: hardly a soul in the morning press tipped Pipedreamer. At the course he was, in a field of nine, a 10/1 outsider. He finished up a 9's. There was only one other horse at a bigger price. Tender Heart was the 5/1 favourite.

Do you find that hard to believe? I certainly did when I looked at the Bookies' Boards. I plunged in like a man possessed; eight separate bets at £50; this would secure that bank for the year. There was a massive crowd at Sandown that lovely afternoon and my bets were hardly noticed in the huge betting market. The bookies had quietly pushed Pipedreamer out from 7/1 in exactly the fashion I described earlier. Like sheep, everyone body-swerved the horse thinking, with the drifting price, heavy weight, and supposed tough track, he had little chance. Fools!

After lying at the rear, Philip Waldron gave him the go-ahead just inside the final furlong. In a few strides Pipedreamer burst clear of his rivals and drew away to win by 3 lengths. It could have been six that afternoon.

Stake	*Return*	*Actual Winnings*	*Bank (c/f £14,374)*
£400	£4,224	£3,824	£18,198

As you will have noticed a few of my recent gambles had gone astray round about this time. Something you must always bear in mind in the latter part of the season is that horses cannot go on for ever. Most of them need a rest sooner or later. Earlier in the week before Pipedreamer's Sandown victory, Northleach at 6/4 was beaten in a lowly handicap at Bath. Because of the price I let him go but, nevertheless, felt he should have won.

About an hour after Pipedreamer's victory House Guard, this time ridden by Tony Kimberley, was beaten by a head at Chester. As you know, I always prefer Piggott for this one and I passed him over too.

All in all, and taking into account the exceptional price I had got about Pipedreamer, I decided it was time to quit for the year. I am no fan of 'back end' racing at all and often in September and October you find some of your short-listed flyers being turned over by late developing horses that, because of poor early-season form, have a big advantage in the weights. This is particularly true of three-year-olds when they take on their older rivals in the latter part of the season. Trying to predict exactly which horses will produce this sudden improvement is a nightmare, especially when the ground softens up again.

One of the most important decisions you have to make in gambling is when to stop. I could have gone on and, in fact, 1979 was a reasonable year to do it in. Northleach, for instance, made a renewed surge later on and won two further races, one at 9/2. House Guard and Piggott snatched another big handicap at Ascot at 7/2 although both Judicial and Strathspey turned out for the same event. Pipedreamer emerged as one of the favourites for the £20,000 William Hill Cambridgeshire Handicap (40+) at Newmarket at the end of September, but predictably his hefty 9 stone 12 lbs. over the straight 9 furlongs, was too much for him. Northleach was unplaced in this race too.

Previous years' records more than anything swayed my final decision. Over the years, bitter experience has taught me that it is often suicidal continuing to back a list of flyers long after many of them have gone off the boil. 1979 certainly illustrates that some of these brave animals *can* keep going but it is really unfair to keep expecting it of them since they are constantly being reviewed and given more and more weight by the handicappers.

Remember! you can stop whenever you feel like it. I made up my mind that Sunday and to ensure no further complications, I baled out to the South of France for six weeks.

APPENDIX

To make things crystal clear for you I have included a chart showing all my bets so that the benefit of the bank idea is clearly imprinted on your brain. You haven't a hope in hell without one.

				Stake	*Return*	*A. Wins.*	*£1,000 Bank*
April 26	Epsom	Black Minstrel	5/1	£ 50	£ 288	£ 238	£ 1,238
April 27	Sandown	Rhyme Royal	11/2	£ 50	£ 312	£ 262	£ 1,500
May 7	Doncaster	Town & Country	—	£ 50	Loser	None	£ 1,450
May 8	Chester	Tesoro Mio	9/1	£ 50	£ 480	£ 430	£ 1,880
May 8	Chester	Black Minstrel	2/1	£ 50	£ 144	£ 94	£ 1,974
May 12	Lingfield	Black Minstrel	—	£ 50	Loser	None	£ 1,924
May 18	Newmarket	House Guard	4/1	£ 50	£ 240	£ 190	£ 2,114 *Doub.*
May 19	Newmarket	Sea Chimes	5/2	£100	£ 336	£ 236	£ 2,350
May 24	Haydock	Black Minstrel	—	£100	Loser	None	£ 2,250
May 28	Sandown	Brians Venture	13/2	£100	£ 720	£ 620	£ 2,870
June 6	Epsom	Tesoro Mio	—	£100	Loser	None	£ 2,770
June 6	Epsom	House Guard	—	£100	Loser	None	£ 2,670
June 8	Epsom	Sea Chimes	5/1	£100	£ 576	£ 476	£ 3,146
June 25	Brighton	So Proper	—	£100	Loser	None	£ 3,046
July 7	Haydock	St. Briavels	7/1	£100	£ 768	£ 668	£ 3714
July 7	Sandown	{ Judicial Red Johnnie }	8/1 —	£100	£ 432	£ 332	£ 4,046 *Doub.*
July 10	Newmarket	Pipedreamer	8/1	£200	£1,728	£1,528	£ 5,574
July 14	York	Tesoro Mio	8/1	£200	£1,728	£1,528	£ 7,102
July 17	Folkestone	Yellow Rock	—	£200	Loser	None	£ 6,902
July 19	Kempton	House Guard	5/2	£200	£ 672	£ 472	£ 7,374
July 21	Ayr	Northleach	9/2	£200	£1,056	£ 856	£ 8,230 *Doub.*
July 25	Sandown	House Guard	5/1	£400	£2,304	£1,904	£10,134
July 26	Sandown	Yellow Rock	—	£400	Loser	None	£9,734
Aug. 2	Goodwood	Northleach	3/1	£400	£1,536	£1,136	£10,870
Aug. 3	Goodwood	Lindoro	2/1	£400	£1,152	£ 752	£11,622
Aug. 4	Newmarket	Judicial	7/2	£400	£1,728	£1,328	£12,950
Aug. 8	Brighton	Yellow Rock	—	£400	Loser	None	£12,550
Aug. 8	Brighton	St. Briavels	—	£400	Loser	None	£12,150
Aug. 11	Redcar	Pipedreamer	—	£400	Loser	None	£11,750
Aug 15	Catterick	Judicial	3/1	£400	£1,536	£1,136	£12,886
Aug. 17	Newbury	Northleach	—	£400	Loser	None	£12,486
Aug. 27	Epsom	Tender Heart	6/1	£400	£2,688	£2,288	£14,774
Aug. 28	Epsom	Palemon	—	£400	Loser	None	£14,374
Sept. 1	Sandown	Pipedreamer	10/1	£400	£4,224	£3,824	£18,198

(34 bets — 21 winners & 13 losers)